MODERN
spanish
COOKING

MODERN spanish COOKING

SAM & EDDIE HART

photography by David Loftus

Publishing director Jane O'Shea
Creative director Helen Lewis
Project editor Janet Illsley
Photographer David Loftus
Food stylists Jean Philippe Patruno
and Nieves Barragán Mohacho
Designer Claire Peters
Production Bridget Fish

This paperback edition first published
in 2006 by Quadrille Publishing Limited
Alhambra House
27–31 Charing Cross Road
London WC2H 0LS
www.quadrille.co.uk

Text © 2006 Sam & Eddie Hart
Photography © 2006 David Loftus,
except pages 26–7 © Sam Bailey
Design and layout © 2006 Quadrille
Publishing Limited

The rights of the authors have been
asserted.

Cataloguing in Publication Data:
a catalogue record for this book is
available from the British Library.

ISBN: 978 184400 454 6

Printed in Singapore

contents

Spoon measures are level unless otherwise stated. 1 tsp = 5ml spoon; 1 tbsp = 15ml spoon.

We only ever use sea salt, preferably Maldon. Where a weight of salt is specified, this refers to Maldon salt. Ordinary table salt is harsher and less would be needed. We also recommend that you use only fresh herbs and freshly ground black pepper unless otherwise suggested.

Olive oil is used in most of our recipes. For a guide to the appropriate olive oil to choose for a particular purpose, refer to the feature on pages 132–3.

We use medium eggs, ideally organic, but always free-range. Anyone who is pregnant or in a vulnerable health group should avoid recipes that use raw or lightly cooked eggs.

Timings are for fan-assisted ovens. If using a conventional oven, increase the temperature by 10–15°C (1/2 Gas mark). Oven settings are often unreliable, so please use an oven thermometer to check the temperature.

Our suggested serving numbers are flexible, depending on the context. For example, tapas can be enlarged to make a light lunch or dinner, or combined with other dishes for a more substantial meal. Equally many of the other dishes can be scaled down to become a tapa.

recipe
NOTES

We have been inspired by Spanish food over the years – both at our family home in the small village of Estellencs in Mallorca and while living in Madrid and Barcelona. Our enthusiasm led us to open our first restaurant, Fino, just off Charlotte Street in central London, three years ago. The style of Spanish food that really inspired us was (and still is) a simple manner of cooking that relies on great produce. There are wonderful markets all over Spain filled with brilliant raw ingredients. Perfectly fresh seafood, tomatoes with a real depth of flavour and truly free-range meat all abound.

You may find our constant reminders of the importance of good quality ingredients somewhat repetitive, but it is the single, most important aspect of all our dishes. At the time Fino opened, Spanish food had a poor reputation in this country but it soon became clear to us that there is a real appetite for Spanish food outside of Spain if it is prepared with top notch ingredients to the highest standards.

We believe it is the strength and clarity of the flavours involved that make Spanish cooking so wonderful. Our philosophy is to seek out a fabulous ingredient and then prepare it in the simplest possible way so that it can really speak for itself. With this style of food you really know what you are eating and the focus on the plate is all on the main ingredient. For us, this makes a happy contrast to the heavily sauced French dishes that all too often lose direction. 'Sourcing not saucing' has become our motto.

While our food is fundamentally simple, it does require careful preparation. When you are cooking this style of food there is nothing to hide behind. Hake cooked 'a la plancha' for example needs to be perfectly fresh, accurately cooked and precisely seasoned. We would urge our readers to source their ingredients carefully, cook accurately and season correctly. With these techniques mastered, successful Spanish cooking comes easily.

We must point out that we are not professional chefs. The demanding skills needed to cook in a busy restaurant kitchen are learnt over many years toiling behind the stoves. Like you, most probably, we are keen amateurs. To this end we must thank our brilliant head chef at Fino, Jean Philippe Patruno, and his sous chef, Nieves Barragán Mohacho for their help with this book. The kitchen at Fino is very much a collaboration between us. In writing this book we feel that being keen amateurs working closely with real professionals has given us the best of both worlds. On the one hand we have been able to pass on truly professional techniques to you, while on the other we have tested our recipes in our own domestic kitchens. Hopefully this means we have addressed the sort of issues you might have in your own kitchen.

Finally, we are firm believers that cooking is as much of an art form as a science. No two pieces of meat will cook in exactly the same way, nor will two ovens apply the same heat. You need to cook with your senses and use your own judgement. Sight, touch, smell and taste are invaluable tools to a cook. We have loved cooking and eating these recipes over the past three years and hope that you will derive similar pleasure from cooking and eating them at home.

Tapas

CERVEZAS
FRESCAS
Y
TAPAS

tapas CULTURE

There are several different stories relating to the origin of tapas, but the one we like best concerns King Alfonso X of Spain (1252–1284). To recuperate from an illness, the king was advised to eat small amounts of food throughout the day. He felt so well on this regime that he decreed that little snacks should be served with wine in all the tavernas throughout the land. The jugs of wine were served with some ham or cheese resting on top, which served the dual purpose of keeping the flies out and keeping customers both sober and healthy.

During the hot summers, the working day started very early in Spain and breakfast would be eaten before dawn. Most of the work would be done in the morning before the heat became too oppressive. A late lunch would follow, then a siesta. To keep them going between breakfast and lunch, workers needed some sustenance, so wine was traditionally served mid-morning along with a simple tapa.

The idea of always having something to nibble on whilst drinking caught on and to this day alcohol is almost always accompanied by something to eat. Traditionally tapas were served free with a drink and were simple – almonds, cheese, olives or slivers of ham. However, as the popularity of tapas grew, so did the variety on offer. Nowadays tapas come in a myriad of different incarnations, from the simple free snack with a drink, to gourmet tapas based on the best ingredients and served in specialist restaurants ... at a price.

For the Spanish, lunch is often still the main meal of the day and in the evening a selection of tapas may therefore suffice. This factor, coupled with the culture of rarely drinking alcohol without food, means that the tapas culture continues to thrive all over Spain. From Barcelona to Seville, Madrid to San Sebastian, young and old mingle together every night in tapas bars to enjoy good food and drink. Spending an evening moving from bar to bar, enjoying a few different dishes in each, is one of life's great pleasures.

When you are on holiday and unfamiliar with the local tapas bars, working out where to go and what to eat can be daunting. Here are our tips to maximise your enjoyment:

The Spanish eat late. Lunch is never before 1.30pm and dinner is not before 9.30pm. **Adapt to Spanish hours**. To do a tapas crawl by oneself while the locals are all asleep is to miss the point.

Often **tapas bars either have no name or** if they do **they are on a street with no name**. Use a map and guidebook to navigate, but be guided more by your instinct and 'gut feel'.

Avoid empty bars and head for the full ones. As with all restaurants the ones that are off the main drag have to work harder to attract clientele. **Try to find busy bars tucked away down little side streets**.

Often a tapas bar will have one or two house specialities. Before ordering have a good look around to see what the locals are eating and **order the most popular dishes first**.

One of the joys of eating tapas is to have a little at a lot of places. **Don't order too much all at once** or you risk being too full to enjoy the best delicacies on offer.

Tread carefully in establishments with a large selection of food on the counter, however good it looks. Usually **the best tapas are cooked to order**. Fried food, such as crispy squid, tastes much better eaten as soon as it is ready.

The Spanish love eating while propping up the bar. Tapas are informal. They are not designed for fancy place settings or tables. The fluidity of the social part of a tapas evening is best enjoyed standing up. **Wear those comfy shoes**.

Finally, **learn Spanish**. Being able to communicate with your hosts is always a good idea.

It is possible to serve a very successful tapas lunch or supper at home provided you plan your menu carefully. Here are our suggestions for tapas-style entertaining:

At the restaurant we serve tapas-sized portions of all dishes to our guests. On average, **people have 3 or 4 dishes each**, so a table of six might order and share as many as 24 different dishes. Obviously if you are cooking tapas for friends at home this number of dishes would be impractical, but you can prepare fewer dishes (increasing the quantities) and extend the meal with a selection of fine Spanish deli foods.

Start with foods that don't need cooking. Spain has a fabulous selection of jamón and other cold meats that demand nothing other than good bread and careful sourcing. The same can be said for other Spanish favourites, such as olives, almonds and cheeses such as Manchego. In addition, there are excellent canned products, including good quality anchovies (both salted and smoked), cockles, mussels in escabeche, etc. These only need a squeeze of lemon, a twist of black pepper and maybe a dash of Tabasco to taste delicious.

Cold soups like Gazpacho (see page 32), marinated fish dishes and most salads can be prepared well ahead of time, leaving you free to concentrate on just a couple of hot dishes. The trick is to **leave yourself very little to do at the last minute**. A selection of fresh seafood cooked 'a la plancha' or crisp-fried is always popular. All you need to do is make a good mayonnaise or alioli in advance and 'plancha' or fry a selection of different seafood at the last moment. Pan con tomate (see page 36, illustrated above left) is a great accompaniment to all sorts of tapas.

Organisation is key to the success of cooking tapas at home. Ideally everything should be perfectly prepped before the first guests arrive. Vegetables should be chopped, meats marinated, fish cleaned and patted dry. Keep your prepared ingredients covered with cling film and leave yourself with a clean kitchen. This way, you will be ready to finish off the dishes quickly as you need to serve them.

We think that a selection of 6–8 prepared dishes should be within the scope of most home cooks, providing the preparation has been done in advance and there is a sensible balance of easy and more difficult dishes. If in doubt keep it simple and bring on the jamón, bread, cheese and olives. In fact we would be happy to dine on just those four items, if of excellent quality, any day of the week!

MARINATED fresh + anchovies

Effectively 'cooked' by the lemon juice and wine vinegar, this is a classic tapa and utterly delicious. We marinate the fish in vinegar for a shorter time than is traditional, to avoid them becoming 'overcooked'. Needless to say, the anchovies or sardines must be very fresh. Get your fishmonger to butterfly the fish for you if possible, removing the backbone and head but keeping both fillets joined together by the tail.

Serves 6

350g large fresh anchovies or very small sardines, cleaned and heads removed
200ml white wine vinegar
juice of 1 lemon
handful of chopped flat leaf parsley
1 garlic clove, peeled and finely chopped
sea salt and freshly ground pepper
about 100ml good extra virgin olive oil

First butterfly the fish (unless the fishmonger has done this for you). Extend the cut along the belly (used for gutting) right down to the tail. Put the anchovies, belly down, on a board and open them out. Press firmly along the backbone with your thumbs to loosen it. Turn the fish over and pull out the backbone. Try to leave the little tail fins on. You will then have the two fillets still joined together.

Wash and carefully dry the anchovies, then place in a shallow dish and pour over the wine vinegar to cover. Leave for about 10 minutes until the anchovies are beginning to turn white, then remove them and pat dry.

Arrange the anchovies, skin side up, in a dish and pour over the lemon juice. Scatter over the chopped parsley and garlic, and season with salt and pepper. Finally drizzle over the olive oil, cover the dish with cling film and refrigerate for 1 hour before serving.

note If you need to clean the anchovies or sardines yourself, simply twist and pinch off the heads, then make a slit along the belly and pull out the innards. Rinse well under cold running water.

crisp FRIED ✚
anchovies

Here are two possibilities for crisp frying anchovies. In the first method, the anchovies are kept whole and dusted in special flour, in the second they are butterflied and fried in a very light batter. Finding fresh anchovies can be tricky in this country, so we are inclined to feast on them when we manage to get some. The preparation is minimal for both methods and it is quite fun to do some of each.

Wash the anchovies under cold running water, then carefully pat dry with kitchen paper. Heat the oil in a deep-fryer or deep saucepan to 180°C. Tip plenty of flour (or mixed flour and breadcrumbs) into a large bowl.

Toss a large handful of anchovies in the flour to coat, gently shake off the excess, then carefully add to the hot oil. Deep-fry for 3 minutes until crisp and golden. Remove with a slotted spoon and drain on kitchen paper. Repeat to cook the rest (in batches).

As soon as they are cooked, sprinkle the anchovies with salt and serve at once, with lemon wedges.

First butterfly the fish (unless the fishmonger has done this for you). Extend the cut along the belly (used for gutting) right down to the tail. Put the anchovies, belly down, on a board and open them out. Press firmly along the backbone with your thumbs to loosen it, then turn the fish over and pull out the backbone. Try to leave the little tail fins on. You will then have the two fillets still joined together. Rinse the anchovy fillets in plenty of cold water, then carefully pat dry.

To make the batter, sift the flour into a mixing bowl and gradually add the water and wine vinegar, whisking until smooth.

Heat the oil in a deep-fryer or deep saucepan to 180°C. Dip a handful of anchovies into the batter to coat, then carefully add them to the hot oil and deep-fry for 3 minutes until crisp and golden. Remove with a slotted spoon and drain on kitchen paper. Repeat to cook the rest (in batches).

As soon as they are cooked, sprinkle the anchovies with salt and serve, with lemon wedges on the side.

Serves 4

method one
250g fresh anchovies, cleaned and heads removed (see note, page 16)
vegetable oil for deep-frying
special flour for frying (see page 22), or equal amounts of plain flour and breadcrumbs mixed together
sea salt
lemon wedges, to serve

method two
250g fresh anchovies, cleaned and heads removed (see note, page 16)
170g plain flour
500ml water
2 tsp white wine vinegar
vegetable oil for deep-frying
sea salt
lemon wedges, to serve

BUÑUELOS DE bacalao

We love salt cod at Fino and this tapa is one of our favourite ways of eating it. Buñuelos are little fritters, which have a crisp outer shell and a wonderful flavour – excellent served with a home-made tartare sauce. Of course, you will need to remember to put the salt cod to soak a day ahead.

Immerse the salt cod in a bowl of cold water and leave to soak in the fridge for 24 hours, changing the water three times.

To make the tartare sauce, whisk the egg yolks and mustard together in a bowl. Mix the oils together and gradually drizzle on to the egg yolk mix, whisking continuously. When all the oil is incorporated, add the shallot, capers and gherkins. Add the lemon juice and mix well, then finally stir in the chopped egg and parsley. Season with salt and pepper to taste. Cover and refrigerate until ready to serve.

Drain the salt cod and cut into 3cm cubes. Place in a saucepan and cover with half milk and half water. Slowly bring to the boil, then remove from the heat and lift the cod out of the pan, discarding the liquid. Crumble the cod with your fingers, carefully removing any bones or skin.

Heat the water and butter together until the butter has melted and the liquid comes to the boil. Take off the heat, immediately add all the flour and beat until smooth. Return to a very low heat and cook for 10 minutes, stirring constantly.

Remove the mixture from the heat and allow to cool for 10 minutes, then beat in the eggs, one at a time, ensuring each egg is incorporated before adding the next. Add the salt cod, garlic, parsley and lemon juice. Mix thoroughly and season to taste. Allow the mixture to cool, then cover and refrigerate for 2 hours.

To shape the buñuelos, either form into quenelles using two dessertspoons, or roll into 3–4cm balls in your hand. Heat the oil in a deep-fryer or deep saucepan to 180°C. Deep-fry the buñuelos in batches for 4–5 minutes until golden and crisp. Drain on kitchen paper and serve immediately, with the tartare sauce.

Makes 20–25

for the buñuelos
500g salt cod
half milk, half water, to cook
250ml water
100g butter
150g plain flour
4 free-range eggs
2 garlic cloves, peeled and crushed
3 tbsp chopped flat leaf parsley
juice of 1 lemon
sea salt and freshly ground pepper
vegetable oil for deep-frying

for the tartare sauce
2 free-range egg yolks
2 tsp Dijon mustard
125ml light olive oil
125ml vegetable oil
1 shallot, peeled and very finely chopped
20g capers, drained and chopped
20g cocktail gherkins, drained and chopped
juice of ½ lemon
1 hard-boiled egg, chopped
1½ tbsp finely chopped flat leaf parsley

QUEEN scallops IN THE shell

We love eating small queen scallops raw and this simple dressing is the perfect foil for their sweetness. We suggest the best way to serve them is chilled, in the shell and on a bed of coarse sea salt. To eat, take the shell in your hands and tip the scallops into your mouth, taking with them a little of the salt from under the shell.

Carefully remove the scallops from their shells with a spoon, reserving the most perfect shells (you need 8–12). Remove the coral and small flap of skin from each scallop. Wash and dry the scallop shells.

Place 2 or 3 cleaned scallops in each shell. Drizzle a little olive oil over them and squeeze 2 or 3 drops of lemon juice into each shell. Carefully add just one drop of Tabasco to each shell. Add a few chopped chives, season with a little salt and pepper and serve immediately.

Serves 4–6

24 fresh queen scallops in the shell
3 tbsp extra virgin olive oil
½ lemon
a little Tabasco (optional)
few chopped chives
sea salt and freshly ground pepper

BACALAO rebozado

This simple fresh cod dish is a favourite of Nieves, our sous chef at Fino. According to Nieves, her mother makes the world's best version at the family home in Bilbao. Unfortunately we have never had the chance to sample her mother's 'bacalao rebozado', but there is certainly something very comforting about this recipe. Try it.

First make the alioli. In a bowl, whisk the egg yolk with the crushed garlic. Then whisk in the olive oil, drop by drop to begin with, then in a steady stream, until it is all emulsified. Season with salt and pepper to taste and set aside.

Cut the cod into 3cm thick slices and carefully pat dry with kitchen paper. Heat the oil in a deep-fryer or deep saucepan to 180°C. Tip the flour into a bowl. Beat the eggs in another bowl with some seasoning.

Dust a large handful of the cod slices in the flour, then dip into the egg to coat and add to the hot oil. Deep-fry for 3–4 minutes until golden, then remove and drain on kitchen paper. Keep warm while you cook the rest (in batches).

Serve at once, with a good dollop of alioli.

Serves 8 (or 4 as a starter)

for the cod
800g cod fillet
vegetable oil for deep-frying
100g plain flour
2 free-range eggs

for the alioli
1 free-range egg yolk
3 garlic cloves, peeled and crushed
100ml light olive oil
sea salt and freshly ground pepper

Perfectly fried squid is always tempting. If possible, buy whole squid with the skin intact and get your fishmonger to clean it for you. A shiny, pink speckled skin is a good indication of freshness. To dust the squid, we use a special flour from southern Spain called 'harina especial para freir', which you can buy from good Spanish delis. Most important of all, be ready to eat the squid the moment it is ready.

crisp FRIED · squid

Serves 8

500g cleaned squid (see note)
vegetable oil for deep-frying
special flour for frying (see above), or
  equal amounts of plain flour and
  breadcrumbs mixed together
sea salt
lemon wedges, to serve

Rinse the squid and carefully pat dry with kitchen paper. Cut the squid into 1.5cm rings and set aside with the tentacles. Heat the oil in a deep-fryer or deep saucepan to 180°C. Tip plenty of flour (or mixed flour and breadcrumbs) into a large bowl.

Cook the squid in batches. Toss a large handful of squid in the flour to coat, gently shake off excess, then carefully add to the hot oil. Deep-fry for 3 minutes until crisp and golden. Remove the squid with a slotted spoon and drain on kitchen paper. Repeat to cook the rest.

As soon as the squid is cooked, sprinkle with a little salt and a tiny drop of lemon juice and eat at once.

note If you need to clean the squid yourself, pull the pouch and tentacles apart and remove the transparent quill from the pouch. Cut the tentacles away from the head just below the eyes and discard the head. Peel off the transparent layer of skin covering the pouch and discard. Rinse the tentacles and the squid pouch thoroughly. Cut the pouch into rings, leaving the tentacles whole.

pulpo
A LA
GALLEGA

Octopus has a reputation for being tricky to cook but, in fact, once you have bought the right beast, it really couldn't be easier. The first thing to look for is an octopus with parallel rows of suckers along its tentacles. These make for better eating than their single sucker cousins. Secondly, it is preferable to buy a frozen octopus, because the freeze/thaw process works as a tenderiser. Octopus from Galicia is frozen in blocks, which doesn't look very appetising, but it springs back to life miraculously when defrosted.

Heat a large saucepan of heavily salted water (as salty as the sea), until boiling. Add the whole octopus, onion and bay leaf, bring back to the boil, then lower the heat to a gentle simmer. Cook for about 45 minutes until tender, but still firm. When prodded with a skewer, the octopus should provide a little resistance. Remove from the pan and leave to cool.

Cut off and discard the head. Slice the tentacles into 2cm rounds. Heat a 2cm depth of olive oil (or enough to cover the octopus) in a saucepan until it registers about 80°C on a cooking thermometer. Add the octopus and cook for about 5 minutes, maintaining a steady heat. The idea is to gently confit the octopus.

Using a slotted spoon, transfer the octopus to a serving dish and spoon over some of the olive oil from the pan. Sprinkle with paprika, a little sea salt and the parsley and serve at once, with some good bread.

Serves 8–10

1 frozen octopus, about 2kg, thawed
sea salt
1 onion, peeled and studded with
* 2 cloves*
1 bay leaf
virgin olive oil for cooking
1–2 tsp sweet paprika
1–2 tbsp chopped flat leaf parsley

THE iberico PIG

Native to Southern Spain, Iberico pigs live in the expansive Mediterranean evergreen oak and cork forests, called the Dehesa. They are distinguishable by their black colour and are smaller than their white cousins, with longer legs. The pigs roam free, rooting around beneath the shady trees and eating acorns. They are reared slowly; it takes about $1 \frac{1}{2}$ years to get them to slaughter weight. Compare this with the typical 18 weeks it takes most commercial pigs to be raised. The special diet and slow rearing gives Iberico pork unique qualities. As the pig's muscles have time to develop properly, the meat is quite red, nearly the colour of lamb, and the fat is marbled throughout the meat, keeping it succulent during cooking. Owing to the acorn-rich diet, this fat has the most wonderful nutty flavour and it has similar cholesterol-reducing properties to olive oil.

Not surprisingly, the Iberico pig lends itself to a range of fine pork products:

The most famous Iberico pork product is the delicious **Jamón Iberico**, which is salted and left to cure for at least a year, sometimes as long as 3 years. The Spanish are justifiably proud of this **'king of hams'** and the names of villages where the hams are cured have taken on almost cult gastronomic status: Jabugo, Teruel, etc. In our opinion, Jamón Iberico is the finest ham in the world and we could happily eat it every day. Come to think of it we do eat it most days!

The naming of Spanish hams is somewhat confusing. There are two main types of ham in Spain: **Jamón Serrano** comes from the more common white pig that is reared by commercial methods, while **Jamón Iberico** comes from the Iberico pig, reared naturally in the Dehesa.

There are **three types of Jamón Iberico**: Jamón Iberico de Bellota – ham from pigs exclusively fattened on acorns; Jamón Iberico de Recebo – from pigs fed on acorns, as well as other foods; and Jamón Iberico de Cebo – from pigs that have lived in the Dehesa but fed on food other than acorns.

Iberico pigs come from three controlled areas: Jamón de Huelva centred round the village of Jabugo; Guijelo in the area around Salamanca; and Dehesa de Extremadura.

So, a jamón from an Iberico pig exclusively fattened on acorns that has been cured in Jabugo would be described as 'Jamón Iberico de Bellota de Jabugo'. Referring to the ham simply as 'Jamón de Jabugo' does not inform you of the breed of the pig or the way it was fattened, both of which are **critical to the quality** of the ham.

Apart from jamón, you can buy **other great Iberico pork products**. Lomo Iberico is the cured loin of the pig, Chorizo Iberico is a paprika-flavoured sausage, Salchichon is a cured sausage without paprika, while Morcilla is a blood sausage that can be either cured or sold raw for cooking.

The fresh meat of the Iberico pig is another huge treat. At Fino, **we use fresh Iberico pork loin that can be safely cooked pink** for Pinchos Morunos (see page 111). We also braise the cheeks of the Iberico pig slowly in red wine (see page 113).

Cured meats such as **jamón and chorizo are available from good Spanish delicatessens**. Sourcing fresh Iberico meat is a little harder. There are several suppliers in the UK and, as we all know, supply results from demand ... a good butcher may respond to pressure.

JAMÓN+ croquetas

We have Fernando, our Madrileño friend, to thank for these. Fernando was very particular about his croquetas and only after 8 months of practice were ours judged to be good enough to eat. The secret is to end up with a béchamel that is only just thick enough to handle; if too thick the croquetas will be stodgy. Ideally, make the béchamel and dry the bread for the crumbs a day ahead.

Make the béchamel a day ahead. Pour the milk into a saucepan, add the bay leaves and slowly bring to the boil. Take off the heat and leave to infuse. Heat the olive oil and butter in a large frying pan, add the jamón cubes and cook over a medium heat for 3–4 minutes. Add the flour and salt, mix well and cook, stirring, for 3 minutes. Remove the bay leaves from the milk, then add it little by little to the roux mix, stirring constantly, for about 10 minutes. When the milk is almost all used, the béchamel should be smooth and thick. Add the rest of the milk and cook for 1 minute.

Pour the thick béchamel on to a large plate or tray, allow to cool, then cover with cling film and refrigerate overnight or for at least 2 hours.

Slice the bread, remove the crusts and leave out to dry overnight. If it isn't dry the following day, place the slices on a tray in the oven at 50°C (lowest setting) for about 30 minutes, but do not allow them to colour.

Break up the bread and whiz to fine crumbs in a blender; tip out on to a plate. Pour the eggs on to another plate. Arrange the béchamel, eggs and breadcrumbs from left to right on your work surface.

To shape the croquetas, using 2 dessertspoons form the béchamel mix into quenelles, about 4cm in length. One at a time, dip the béchamel quenelles into the beaten egg, then coat in the breadcrumbs. Gently shape the croquetas by rolling them between your cupped hands, applying more breadcrumbs to cover any bare patches. Carefully place them on a plate. Repeat to use all of the mixture, then chill in the fridge for about 20 minutes.

Heat the oil in a deep-fryer or deep saucepan to 180°C and cook the croquetas, 4 or 5 at a time. Carefully immerse in the hot oil and deep-fry for 2–3 minutes. Remove and drain on kitchen paper. Serve the croquetas straight away.

variation

cep croquetas You can make these in the same way, replacing the jamón with 300g fresh ceps or other flavourful wild mushrooms.

Makes 40

for the béchamel
500ml whole milk
2 bay leaves
4 tsp good quality light olive oil
80g slightly salted butter
125g jamón Serrano cubes or strips
70g plain flour
pinch of sea salt

for the breadcrumbs
1 small loaf of good quality white bread
4 free-range eggs, beaten

for frying
500ml vegetable or groundnut oil

girolles AND jamón

This dish is extremely simple to prepare, yet delicious. If you happen to have a leg of jamón, then this is the perfect way to use your offcuts. Otherwise ask your butcher or delicatessen to cut cubes rather than slices of jamón as this will keep the meat from drying out.

Serves 4–6

*500g girolles or other wild
  mushrooms, cleaned
3 tbsp light olive oil
1 shallot, peeled and finely chopped
1 garlic clove, peeled and finely sliced
100g jamón, cut into 5mm cubes
sea salt and freshly ground pepper
1 tbsp finely chopped flat leaf parsley*

Halve or quarter any larger mushrooms. Heat the olive oil in a large frying pan and add the mushrooms. Cook, tossing the mushrooms, over a medium high heat for 3 minutes. Add the shallot and garlic and sauté for a further minute.

Remove from the heat and add the jamón. Toss to mix and season with salt and pepper to taste. Sprinkle with the chopped parsley and serve immediately.

+ JAMÓN consommé

We think this is one of the greatest consommés in the world. Whenever you have a jamón at home, this puts the bone to good use. Alternatively, you can buy a ham bone from a Spanish deli. For a really clear consommé, you'll need to strain the clarified stock through a sieve lined with muslin, or you could pass it through a very fine sieve several times. Serve small portions in little cups as a tapa, or standard portions in bowls as a starter. The consommé is also a brilliant addition to many other dishes, especially broad beans and jamón (see page 139), and lentil dishes; you can also use it to make a sauce for grilled pork.

Serves 12 as a tapa (6 as a starter)

2 tbsp light olive oil
1.5kg jamón bones, chopped into 10cm lengths
1 onion, peeled and chopped
1 leek, trimmed and chopped
2 celery sticks, chopped
1 bay leaf
3 tomatoes, chopped

for the clarifying mix
3 free-range egg whites (shells reserved)
300g minced lean pork

to serve
chives

Heat the olive oil in a large stockpot or pan and fry the ham bones until they take on a little colour, about 10 minutes.

Add the vegetables, bay leaf and tomatoes, then pour in enough water to just cover. Bring to the boil, skim off any impurities that rise to the surface, then reduce the heat to a low simmer. Cook for $2\frac{1}{2}$ hours, skimming every so often. Pass the stock through a fine sieve 3 or 4 times. Leave to cool.

For the clarifying mix, blitz the egg whites and their shells with the minced pork in a blender.

Return the jamón stock to a medium heat and whisk in the clarifying mix. Bring to the boil, then lower the heat and gently simmer for about 20 minutes. Carefully strain the liquid through a muslin-lined sieve into a clean pan. Taste the consommé and simmer to reduce if it is not strong enough, or add some water if it is too salty. The salt content of the bones determines the extent to which you can reduce the consommé. The aim is to get to the point where the consommé is perfectly seasoned.

Ladle the hot consommé into coffee cups or small bowls, sprinkle with a few chives and serve at once.

In hot weather, we can happily start every meal with a little cup of this delicious chilled gazpacho. At Fino, we only serve it during the few months of the year when we can find tomatoes that really taste of something. After all, this is a tomato soup and unless the tomatoes you use are good ones, the exercise is pointless. Find a good greengrocer and only make gazpacho when tomatoes are in season and flavourful.

gazpacho

Put the tomatoes, spring onions, garlic and cucumber in a blender and whiz to a purée. Pass through a fine sieve 2 or 3 times. Return the mixture to the blender and, with the motor running, slowly add the olive oil through the feeder funnel.

Add the sherry vinegar, then season with salt and pepper to taste. Pour into a jug or bowl, cover and refrigerate for at least 2 hours.

In the meantime, prepare the garnish. Finely dice all the vegetables and the hard-boiled egg.

To make croûtons, remove the crusts from the bread, then cut into 1cm cubes. Heat a thin film of olive oil in a frying pan, add the bread cubes and fry gently, turning until evenly golden and crisp. Drain on kitchen paper.

Ladle the soup into cups or bowls, drizzle with a little olive oil and grind a little pepper over the top if you like. Serve the garnish on the side, so everyone can help themselves.

Serves 8 as a tapa (4 as a starter)

1kg tomatoes
4 spring onions, trimmed
3 garlic cloves, peeled
½ cucumber
75ml virgin olive oil
25ml sherry vinegar
sea salt and freshly ground pepper

for the garnish
2 spring onions, trimmed
½ red pepper, cored and deseeded
½ green pepper, cored and deseeded
½ cucumber
1 hard-boiled egg
1–2 slices of bread
olive oil for frying
finest extra virgin olive oil, to drizzle

salmorejo

Salmorejo is a variation of the more renowned Gazpacho. Salmorejo does not use cucumber or peppers but it does use chopped egg and jamón. There is nothing more delicious on a hot day accompanied by a glass or two of ice-cold Manzanilla or Fino sherry, or even a bottle of Taxcoli, a fresh white wine from the Basque Country.

Serves 12 (or 6 as a starter)

*200g good quality white bread
  (sourdough), crusts removed
1kg very ripe, flavourful tomatoes
4 garlic cloves, peeled and finely diced
1 tsp sherry vinegar
sea salt and freshly ground pepper
4–6 tbsp extra virgin olive oil*

for the garnish

*1 hard-boiled egg, chopped
125g jamón Serrano, diced
4 tsp flat leaf parsley, finely chopped
finest extra virgin olive oil, to drizzle*

Soak the bread in cold water to cover for about 10 minutes, then remove and squeeze out the excess water. Meanwhile, briefly dip the tomatoes, a few at a time, into very hot water to loosen the skins, then peel. Halve the tomatoes and cut out the stalk ends.

Put the tomatoes, garlic, sherry vinegar, bread and a good pinch of sea salt in a blender and whiz to a smooth consistency. Then, with the motor running, add the olive oil in a thin stream through the feeder funnel. Check the seasoning, adding pepper to taste. Pour into a bowl or jug, cover and chill in the fridge for at least 2 hours.

Ladle the soup into bowls or cups. Sprinkle with the chopped egg, jamón and parsley, and add a drizzle of extra virgin olive oil.

ajo ✛
BLANCO

We always thought this cold soup from Andalucia would taste disgusting until we tried it! We became converts at once. The Spanish are experts on almonds and have many different varieties and grades – try to find the best you can. We quite like an espresso cup serving of this chilled soup as a tapa or little snack, but you can serve more as a starter.

Soak the bread in milk to cover for 10 minutes or so, then remove and squeeze out the excess milk. Put the apples, almonds, garlic, bread and water in a blender and whiz until smooth. Transfer the soup to a bowl or jug, cover and refrigerate for at least 2 hours.

When you are ready to eat, return the soup to the blender. Then, with the motor running, slowly add the olive oil and sherry vinegar through the feeder tube. Season with salt and pepper to taste.

Ladle the soup into cups or bowls and sprinkle with the diced apple, raisins and pine nuts. Drizzle a little fine olive oil on top of each portion and serve at once.

Serves 12 (or 6 as a starter)

3 slices of day-old white bread, crusts
  removed
a little milk
3 apples, peeled, quartered and cored
200g blanched almonds
4 garlic cloves, peeled
600ml water
150ml olive oil
4 tsp sherry vinegar
sea salt and freshly ground pepper

for the garnish
1 apple, peeled and diced
30g raisins
30g pine nuts, lightly toasted
finest extra virgin olive oil, to drizzle

pimientos DE PADRÓN

The best way to enjoy these delicious little green capsicums from Padrón and Herbón in Galicia is to eat them as a tapa – fried in olive oil and sprinkled with a generous pinch of sea salt. Great mystery enshrouds Padrón pimientos for although most are mild and sweet, one in ten is guaranteed to knock your socks off! Almost every Spaniard purports to have their own way of identifying the hot ones, but unless you come from one of the hundred or so Padrón-producing families, we think it is almost impossible to tell. Be brave and ensure there is always a cold glass of Manzanilla on standby …

Serves 4–6

200g pimientos de Padrón
2 tbsp good quality light olive oil
4 large pinches of sea salt

Wash the peppers thoroughly in cold water and pat dry. Place a large frying pan (which has a lid) over a high heat, add the olive oil and heat until smoking. Add the peppers, cover and cook for 4–5 minutes, turning occasionally, until blistered and slightly charred.

Drain the peppers on kitchen paper, sprinkle generously with the salt and serve.

pan CON tomate

This classic Catalan dish is eaten at nearly every meal throughout the region. It was originally devised to refresh stale bread and to use up a surplus of tomatoes (almost inevitable if you grow your own). Served on its own or with cold meats or marinated anchovies, pan con tomate is simple and delicious. When on holiday at our house in Mallorca, we eat this every day for breakfast. The secret is to use great tomatoes, delicious olive oil and really good bread. (Illustrated on page 14)

Cut the bread into 1–2cm thick slices and toast until lightly browned. Halve the garlic clove(s) if using and rub the cut side gently on to the toast while it is still hot.

Rub the cut side of a tomato half over the toast so that the juice and seeds pour out over the top. Discard the rest of the tomato.

Drizzle with olive oil, sprinkle with chopped parsley if you like, and season with salt and pepper. Serve at once.

Serves 6

1 loaf of good quality, crusty bread
3 garlic cloves, unpeeled (optional)
6 tomatoes (the ripest and sweetest you can find), halved
100ml good quality olive oil
2 tbsp chopped flat leaf parsley (optional)
sea salt and freshly ground pepper

Rice, Beans & Eggs

This is very similar to a paella but with rather more 'soup'. Certainly, having a little sauce to mop up seems to add to the comfort factor. In Catalunya, you will see locals eating this dish almost as often as paella. The seafood you use can be varied, according to what is available at the time.

Serves 4

for the stock

1½ tbsp olive oil
1kg white fish head and/or bones
reserved prawn shells and heads
  (see recipe)
1 onion, peeled and finely chopped
1 fennel bulb, trimmed and finely
  chopped
2 celery sticks, finely chopped
2 tbsp tomato purée
1 tsp Spanish hot smoked paprika
125ml brandy
250ml white wine or Fino sherry
1¾ litres water
pinch of saffron threads
5 tsp sea salt

for the seafood rice

250g raw small prawns, heads on
4 raw large prawns or langoustines,
  heads on, cleaned
250g monkfish fillet
250g squid, cleaned (see page 22)
1½ tbsp olive oil
1 onion, peeled and finely chopped
6 garlic cloves, peeled and finely
  chopped
400g Bomba or Calasparra rice
  (paella rice)
400g fresh mussels, cockles or clams
  (or a mixture), cleaned

to serve

lemon wedges
alioli (optional, see page 70)

First remove the heads and shells from the small prawns and reserve for the stock. Refrigerate the prawns, with the whole large prawns.

For the stock, heat the olive oil in a large, heavy-based saucepan. Add the fish head and bones with the prawn shells and heads. Fry over a medium heat for 20 minutes, stirring and mashing all the while. Add the onion, fennel and celery and cook for 5 minutes. Stir in the tomato purée and paprika and cook for 10 minutes. Pour in the brandy and wine and bring to the boil. Take off the heat and carefully ignite with a long match to burn off the alcohol. Return to the heat and reduce by half. Add the water, saffron and salt. Bring to the boil, then lower the heat and simmer gently for 45 minutes, skimming the surface from time to time. Pass the stock through a fine sieve 3 or 4 times, then set aside.

Cut the monkfish into 2cm medallions. Cut the squid pouches into 1cm rings, reserving the tentacles. Set aside with the prawns.

Heat the olive oil in a large, heavy-based frying pan or paella pan. Add the onion and fry over a medium heat for 10 minutes until softened. Add the garlic and squid and fry for another 5 minutes. Add the rice, stir well and fry for 3 minutes until translucent. Add almost all of the stock and bring to the boil, then reduce the heat to a vigorous simmer and cook for 10 minutes. Don't stir the rice, but every so often, give the pan a little shake to make sure it doesn't stick.

Add the monkfish, prawns and mussels to the pan, arranging them attractively as you won't be stirring any more. Cook for another 8 minutes until the mussel shells have opened; discard any that remain closed. You now have to decide whether to add more stock. Taste the rice – it should be nearly ready – then add more stock if needed. You are aiming for a slightly soupy consistency when the rice is completely cooked, but not for the dish to be too liquid.

Let the dish rest for 5 minutes, then serve with lemon wedges and good bread for mopping up the liquor. You could also serve a big bowl of alioli on the side if you like.

ARROZ negro

We believe that the secret to really good 'black rice' is plenty of ink. Too often the rice is rather more grey than black. The addition of butter at the end is somewhat unorthodox, but in our view improves the dish. You can serve the rice simply as it is, or garnished with pan-fried squid as shown.

Serves 4 (or 8 as starter)

220g cleaned squid (see page 22)
3 tbsp olive oil
4 spring onions, trimmed and finely
  chopped
350ml Fino or Manzanilla sherry
2 shallots, peeled and finely diced
1 litre fish stock (see page 44,
  omitting the prawn shells and heads)
350g Bomba or Arborio rice
8 sachets of squid ink
large knob of butter
sea salt and freshly ground pepper

to serve

2 small squid, cleaned (optional)
2 tsp light olive oil (optional)
small handful of flat leaf parsley,
  chopped (optional)
extra virgin olive oil, to drizzle
lemon wedges

Dice the prepared squid. Heat half the olive oil in a large, heavy-based frying pan and fry the squid until golden and all the liquid has evaporated. Add the spring onions and 150ml sherry and let bubble until the sherry has reduced totally. Remove from the pan and set aside.

Heat the remaining olive oil in the pan and gently fry the shallots for 10 minutes until softened and golden. Meanwhile, bring the stock to a simmer in another pan and keep it at a low simmer.

Add the rice to the shallots and fry for 2–3 minutes, then pour in the rest of the sherry and stir to deglaze. Add a couple of ladlefuls of stock and cook, stirring every so often, until the liquid is absorbed. Continue to add stock in this way until the rice is nearly cooked.

In the meantime, prepare the garnish if required. Slice the squid pouches into rings, keeping the tentacles whole. Heat the olive oil in a frying pan, add the squid and pan-fry for a few minutes until tender. Throw in the chopped parsley and set aside.

Add the squid ink to the rice, with a little more stock if necessary, and stir well. At this stage the rice should be perfectly cooked. Stir in a large knob of butter and season with salt and pepper to taste.

Serve the rice in warm bowls, drizzled with extra virgin olive oil and topped with the pan-fried squid if using. Serve with lemon wedges.

Paella comes in many forms, and in our experience the quality is variable. Hopefully, as you enjoy this recipe on a terrace or in a garden with plenty of cold rosé, you'll appreciate why this is one of Spain's most revered dishes. Unlike a risotto, a paella should have a nutty rather than a creamy consistency and should not be stirred. If you're concerned that the rice is sticking, give the pan a good shake and turn down the heat a little. Expert paella cooks manage to achieve a 'crocant' or crisp layer on the bottom – this is the best bit. The heat must be just right, so that the rice is ready as the last of the stock evaporates. Then it will fry and crisp a little on the bottom, without burning. Practise makes perfect!

SEAFOOD paella +

First, remove the heads and shells from the prawns and save for the stock. Refrigerate the prawns until you are ready to make the paella.

To make the stock, heat the olive oil in a very large saucepan or stockpot. Add the prawn heads and shells and cook for 1–2 minutes, breaking them down with a wooden spoon. Add the onion and fennel and sweat over a medium heat for 10–15 minutes until starting to caramelise. Add the tomato purée, tomatoes and paprika and cook for 5 minutes, stirring. Add the brandy, take off the heat and carefully ignite to burn off the alcohol. Return to the heat and stir with a wooden spoon to deglaze.

Add the thyme, bay leaves and water. Bring to the boil, then lower the heat. Simmer until reduced almost by half (to about 1.1 litres); this will take about 45 minutes–1 hour. Strain the stock through a sieve into a jug, season generously with salt and some pepper and keep to one side.

To make the paella, place a 34cm paella pan over a medium heat, add the olive oil and fry the onion for 2 minutes. Add the peppers with a pinch of salt and fry for 2 minutes. Add the garlic and fry for a further 2 minutes. Add the bay leaves and squid and cook, stirring, for 4 minutes. Add the paprika and cook, stirring, for 2 minutes.

Add the rice, mix well and cook for 2 minutes. Add the saffron, pour in 1 litre of the stock, increase the heat and bring back to the boil. Simmer vigorously for 10 minutes.

Add the prawns, placing them in a ring towards the middle of the pan. Add the mussels and clams, pushing them down into the rice. Cook for a further 8 minutes. If the paella appears to be drying out before it is cooked, ladle a little more stock over the rice, always remembering that you are aiming for a dry (not a soupy) result. For the last 5 minutes or so, there won't be much stock in the pan.

Take off the heat, cover with foil and leave the paella to rest in a warm place for 5 minutes. The steam will cook the rice on the top, which might be a little underdone before resting. Remove the foil, scatter with parsley and drizzle with extra virgin olive oil. Serve at once, with lemon wedges.

Serves 4–6

for the stock
3 tbsp light olive oil
prawn shells and heads (see recipe)
1 onion, peeled and diced
1 fennel bulb, trimmed and diced
4 tsp tomato purée
3 plum tomatoes, diced
1 tsp smoked sweet paprika
125ml brandy
bunch of thyme sprigs
2 bay leaves
2 litres water
sea salt and freshly ground pepper

for the paella
500g (8 large) raw tiger prawns or
   langoustines, cleaned
3 tbsp good quality light olive oil
1 large onion, peeled and finely diced
1 each red and green peppers, cored,
   deseeded and diced
3 garlic cloves, peeled and sliced
2 bay leaves
250g squid, cleaned and cut into rings
   (see page 22)
1 tsp sweet paprika
400g Bomba or Calasparra rice
   (paella rice)
2 small pinches of saffron threads
300g fresh mussels, cleaned
300g fresh clams, cleaned

to serve
handful of flat leaf parsley, chopped
4 tsp good quality extra virgin olive oil
lemon wedges

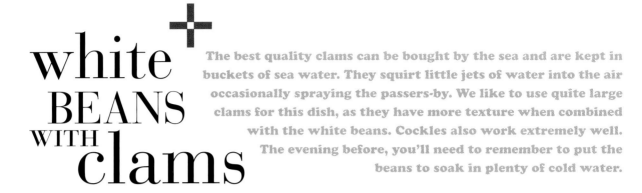

white BEANS WITH clams

The best quality clams can be bought by the sea and are kept in buckets of sea water. They squirt little jets of water into the air occasionally spraying the passers-by. We like to use quite large clams for this dish, as they have more texture when combined with the white beans. Cockles also work extremely well. The evening before, you'll need to remember to put the beans to soak in plenty of cold water.

Drain the soaked beans and rinse well under cold running water. Place in a large saucepan with the celery, leek and 1 carrot, then add plenty of cold water to cover generously. Bring to the boil, then lower the heat and simmer for $1^{1}/_{2}$–2 hours until the beans are tender, but not so soft that they start to fall apart. Remove and discard the vegetables, then drain the beans, keeping 100ml of the cooking liquor.

Cut the fennel and remaining carrot into 1cm cubes and set aside with the shallots. Heat 1 tbsp olive oil in a large saucepan until smoking. Add the clams, 100ml of the sherry and the thyme sprigs and cover with a tight-fitting lid. Cook for between 30 seconds and 1 minute until the clam shells open, then remove from the heat. When the clams have cooled a little, carefully remove them from their shells and put to one side, with their cooking juices.

Heat the remaining 2 tbsp olive oil in a large frying pan and fry the shallots, fennel, carrot, garlic and bacon lardons over a high heat for 2–3 minutes. Add the fish stock, reserved bean cooking liquor and remaining sherry, stirring to deglaze for 1–2 minutes until the liquid comes back to the boil. Add the white beans and cook for a further 2 minutes. Add the chopped tomatoes and cook for another minute.

Remove from the heat and add the parsley and clams together with their cooking juices. Turn the mixture several times, seasoning with salt and pepper and adding lemon juice to taste as you do so. Drizzle with extra virgin olive oil and serve.

Serves 4

200g dried white beans
  (alubias, arrocina or haricot blancs),
  soaked overnight
1 celery stick
1 leek, trimmed
2 carrots, peeled
$^{1}/_{2}$ fennel bulb, trimmed
2 shallots, peeled and finely chopped
3 tbsp good quality olive oil
500g fresh clams, cleaned
200ml Fino or Manzanilla sherry
3 thyme sprigs
2 garlic cloves, peeled and finely
  chopped
50g bacon or jamón lardons
100ml fish stock (see page 44,
  omitting the prawn shells and heads)
3 tomatoes, peeled, deseeded and cut
  into 1cm squares
1 tbsp roughly chopped flat leaf parsley
sea salt and freshly ground pepper
juice of $^{1}/_{2}$ lemon, or to taste
2 tbsp extra virgin olive oil, to drizzle

white BEANS
AND
✛ morcilla

Morcilla is a Spanish blood sausage and, in our view, delicious. Although fairly rich, there is nothing challenging about its flavour. We first ate this dish as a late breakfast at Bar Pinotxo in the middle of Barcelona's Boqueria market. The secret is to have quite a lot of morcilla in relation to beans. For this recipe you should use morcillas made with onion, rather than those made with rice. You will need to soak the beans overnight.

Serves 4

200g dried white beans
  (alubias, arrocina or haricot blancs),
  soaked overnight
6 tbsp light olive oil
1 onion, peeled and finely diced
4 garlic cloves, peeled and finely
  chopped
4 onion morcilla sausages, skinned
sea salt and freshly ground pepper
handful of flat leaf parsley, chopped
extra virgin olive oil, to drizzle

Drain the soaked beans and rinse well under cold running water. Place in a large saucepan and add plenty of cold water to cover. Bring to the boil, then lower the heat and simmer for $1\frac{1}{2}$–2 hours until the beans are tender, but still holding their shape. Drain the beans and set aside.

Heat the olive oil in a large, heavy-based saucepan over a medium heat and fry the onion for 10 minutes. Add the garlic and fry for another 2 minutes. Add the morcillas and cook, mashing and stirring, until evenly blended with the onion and garlic. Add the beans, season with salt and pepper and fry for 5 minutes.

Remove from the heat, check the seasoning and stir in the chopped parsley. Drizzle with extra virgin olive oil and serve with plenty of good bread, and perhaps an icy cold beer.

+ lentejas

Put the lentils in a large saucepan or stockpot with 1 carrot, roughly chopped, the celery, onion, leek, bay leaves and thyme. Add cold water to cover generously and bring to the boil. Lower the heat and simmer for 50 minutes. Drain the lentils and discard the vegetables and herbs.

Heat the olive oil in a large frying pan over a medium heat. Add the shallot, garlic and chorizo and fry for 2–3 minutes. Add the morcilla and paprika and fry for a further 2–3 minutes. Remove from the heat.

Return the lentils to the large pan or stockpot and add the chorizo and morcilla mixture. Add enough water to cover by about 4cm and bring to the boil. Lower the heat to a simmer and cook for 20 minutes.

Add the new potatoes, season with salt and pepper, and simmer for a further 30 minutes. If necessary during cooking, add a ladleful of water to keep the lentils wet.

In the meantime, finely dice the rest of the carrots. Add them to the lentils and cook for a further 5 minutes. Check the seasoning, divide between warm bowls and serve.

Serves 6–8

500g Puy lentils
300g large carrots, peeled
2 celery sticks, roughly chopped
½ Spanish onion, peeled
1 leek, trimmed and roughly chopped
2 bay leaves
4 thyme sprigs
3 tbsp light olive oil
1 shallot, peeled and finely sliced
1 garlic clove, peeled and thinly sliced
300g cooking chorizo sausage, cut into 2cm slices
300g morcilla sausage, skinned and cut into 2cm slices
1 tsp sweet paprika
300g baby new potatoes (unpeeled)
sea salt and freshly ground pepper

We first tasted this dish with Pep Manubens at his restaurant Cal Pep in Barcelona. Perched at the eating bar, we were amazed and delighted by the flavours and simplicity. Buy the best quality pancetta or bacon you can find. If you use watery bacon, which is standard in most supermarkets, the most troubling quantity of scum will surface as you cook the chickpeas. You will need to remember to soak the chickpeas overnight.

chickpeas, SPINACH AND + bacon

Serves 4

350g dried chickpeas, soaked overnight
1.6 litres water
1 onion, peeled and roughly chopped
1 celery stick, roughly chopped
1 leek, trimmed and roughly chopped
2 bay leaves
bunch of thyme sprigs
400g pancetta or bacon lardons
3 tbsp light olive oil
1 banana shallot, peeled and finely
  chopped
1 garlic clove, peeled and finely
  chopped
150g baby spinach, washed and
  drained
sea salt and freshly ground pepper

Drain the chickpeas and place in a large saucepan with the water. Add the onion, celery, leek, bay leaves, thyme and 200g of the pancetta. Bring to the boil over a high heat and then lower the heat to a simmer. Cook for 50 minutes or until the chickpeas are perfectly cooked – soft but not disintegrating. Drain the chickpeas, reserving the liquid, and set aside.

Heat the olive oil in a large saucepan over a medium heat and add the remaining pancetta with the shallot. Sweat gently for 3–4 minutes, then add the garlic and sweat for a further 2 minutes.

Add the baby spinach and sweat for 1 minute until just wilted. Add the chickpeas and 2 tbsp of the reserved stock. Bring back to the boil, then remove from the heat and season with salt and pepper to taste. Serve immediately.

Discussing the best and correct way to execute a certain classic dish with the Spanish always evokes great passion and decisiveness. You will normally be informed that there is only one way and that recipe belongs to their family or, more importantly, to their grandmother. This has often left us slightly mystified and no more so than with this Madrid staple.

The secret of a good 'cocido madrileno' is to end up with perfectly cooked meat and a tasty soup. If after the recommended cooking time, the soup is not tasty enough, remove the meat and vegetables and reduce the liquor over a high heat to concentrate the flavour, then put everything back together again. You will need to soak the chickpeas overnight.

cocido + MADRILENO

Serves 6–8

500g dried chickpeas, soaked overnight
4 tbsp light olive oil
500g shoulder of beef, cut into
  3cm cubes
125g tocino or pork back fat, or
  smoked bacon lardons
100g jamón Serrano lardons
4 organic or free-range chicken thighs
2 cooking chorizo sausages
2 onion morcilla sausages
2 bay leaves
2 marrow bones
2 onions, peeled and quartered
3 carrots, peeled and quartered
  lengthways
3 garlic cloves, peeled and smashed
6 baby turnips, peeled
500g medium potatoes (about 4),
  peeled and cut into small chunks
sea salt and freshly ground pepper
1 Savoy cabbage, cored and finely
  shredded

Preheat the oven to 180°C/Gas 4. Drain the chickpeas and set aside. Heat the olive oil in a very large flameproof casserole or heavy-based saucepan over a high heat. First add the shoulder of beef, then the pork fat, jamón lardons, chicken thighs, chorizos and morcillas and brown lightly for 10 minutes.

Add the chickpeas to the casserole with the bay leaves. Add enough cold water to cover everything by about 4cm and bring to the boil. Skim any impurities from the surface of the cocido and reduce the heat. Simmer gently for 1 1/2 hours.

After the cocido has been simmering for 40 minutes or so, lay the marrow bones in a roasting pan and put into the oven to roast.

Add the onions, carrots, garlic and turnips to the chickpeas and cook for 15 minutes. Add the potatoes and a little seasoning and cook for 5 minutes, then add the cabbage and simmer for a further 10 minutes or until the potatoes are tender. Check the seasoning.

Using a slotted spoon, take out the chicken, chorizos, morcillas and pork fat and divide between warm serving bowls, cutting the sausages and pork fat into portions to do so. Remove the marrow bones from the oven and place one in each bowl. Add a generous ladleful of the cocido to each bowl and enjoy, with crusty bread.

+ huevos
ESCALFADOS

This simple egg dish makes a delicious Sunday evening supper. The Romesco sauce goes brilliantly with the poached eggs and toasted almonds. Use the very best eggs you can find.

First, make the Romesco sauce. Preheat the oven to 140°C/Gas 1. Soak the dried red peppers and chilli in warm water to cover for about 10 minutes, then drain. Put 3 tbsp light olive oil in a shallow roasting pan, add the almonds and garlic cloves, toss to coat in the oil and roast for 10 minutes, taking care not to burn the nuts. Transfer to a plate and set aside. Increase the oven setting to 180°C/Gas 4.

Heat a thin film of light olive oil in a frying pan and fry the bread slices on both sides until golden brown. Drain on kitchen paper and keep to one aside. Place the tomatoes in the roasting pan, drizzle with 3 tbsp light olive oil and roast for 15–20 minutes. Let cool slightly.

Tip the roasted tomatoes, nuts and garlic into a blender and whiz to a purée. With the motor running, add the bread slices, one at a time, followed by the soaked peppers and chilli, then the sherry vinegar. Continue to blend as you drizzle in the extra virgin olive oil. Season with salt and pepper to taste, transfer to a bowl and keep to one side.

For the eggs, spread the almonds on a roasting tray and toast in the oven for 10 minutes or until golden brown.

Half-fill a large frying pan with water, bring to the boil and reduce the heat to a gentle simmer. Crack an egg into a ladle, gently lower into the water and hold for 1 minute, then slide into the simmering water and cook for 3 minutes. Repeat with the rest of the eggs (so you are adding them at 1–minute intervals). As each poached egg is cooked, carefully remove it with a slotted spoon and pat dry with kitchen paper.

Place the eggs on warm plates and sprinkle with the toasted almonds, spring onions and chopped parsley. Serve at once, with the Romesco sauce on the side.

Serves 4

for the eggs

60g skinned almonds

4 very fresh duck eggs or free-range
  hen's eggs

2 spring onions, trimmed and finely
  sliced into rounds

2 tsp finely chopped flat leaf parsley

for the romesco sauce

2 dried red peppers

1 dried red chilli

light olive oil for cooking

40g skinned almonds or hazelnuts
  (or a mixture)

3 garlic cloves, peeled

3 slices of best quality white bread,
  crusts removed

1kg tomatoes

2 tbsp sherry vinegar

4 tbsp extra virgin olive oil

sea salt and freshly ground pepper

tortilla +
ESPANOLA

Nothing can surpass a perfect tortilla. The secret is to have lots of wonderfully caramelised onion and potato mixed with a relatively small amount of egg. Don't be tempted to rush the frying of the onions and potatoes, as they need to caramelise slowly for optimum flavour. The end result also depends on using the finest quality eggs you can find. We like to cook individual tortillas in non-stick blini pans but you can, of course, cook a big one in a large, heavy-based, non-stick frying pan.

Heat a 1–1.5cm depth of olive oil in a deep, medium frying pan. Add the onions and cook slowly for about 30 minutes until soft and golden. In the meantime, peel the potatoes and slice into 1cm rounds.

Add the potatoes to the onions and turn up the heat a little. Cook until the potatoes are soft and golden, but not crispy, breaking them up with the spatula and stirring the mixture frequently. When the mixture has become a dark brown mush, take off the heat and drain well on kitchen paper. Let cool slightly.

Beat the eggs in a bowl. Add the potato and onion mix and season well with salt and pepper. Heat 1 tsp olive oil in a non-stick blini pan over a medium heat and add a sixth of the mixture. Cook for about 2 minutes, gently pushing the back of the spatula around the edge of the tortilla to create a rounded edge.

Invert the tortilla on to a plate, then slide back into the pan and cook on the other side for $1^{1}/_{2}$–2 minutes – it should still be nice and runny in the middle. Turn out on to a warm plate; keep warm. Repeat to make the rest of the tortillas, then serve at once. We prefer to eat tortilla hot, but a good tortilla will also be enjoyable cold or at room temperature.

Serves 6

light olive oil for cooking
700g onions, peeled and finely sliced
700g ordinary white potatoes
5 fine quality free-range eggs
sea salt and freshly ground pepper

variations

spinach tortilla Cook 100g fresh baby spinach leaves in a little olive oil for a minute or two until wilted, cool slightly, then add to the egg, potato and onion mix before cooking the tortillas.

chorizo tortilla Cut 2 picante or other cooking chorizo sausages into small cubes and fry in a little oil for 2–3 minutes until cooked. Drain, cool slightly and add to the egg with the potato and onion. Cook the tortillas as above and serve topped with a good dollop of alioli (see page 70).

brown shrimp tortilla Add 150g chopped peeled brown shrimp and a small handful of chopped garlic tops or chives to the beaten eggs.

morcilla + AND duck egg

Heat 2 tbsp of the olive oil in a frying pan and add the morcillas. Cook for a minute or two, breaking up the sausages with a spatula.

Heat the rest of the olive oil in another pan and carefully break the eggs into the pan. As they fry, spoon the hot oil over the top of the eggs to ensure the yolks cook. Share out the hot morcilla between four warm plates and place a fried egg on top of each portion.

Sprinkle the paprika into the morcilla pan, stir and then pour a little of this flavoured oil on top of each egg. Season the egg with salt and pepper, sprinkle with a little chopped parsley and serve with good bread.

Serves 4

3 tbsp light olive oil
400g morcilla sausages, skinned
4 duck eggs, or free-range hen's eggs
1 tsp sweet paprika
sea salt and freshly ground pepper
1–2 tbsp chopped flat leaf parsley

SCRAMBLED + egg WITH truffles

We always get excited at the start of both the white and black truffle seasons. In our opinion, truffles are best combined with the simplest ingredients such as eggs, pasta or rice. For this very simple dish, it is imperative that you find really good eggs – ideally from an enthusiastic small producer. You can get away with using less truffle, but not so little that the point of the dish is lost.

Serves 4

1 fresh black truffle, about 30g
12 finest free-range eggs
sea salt and freshly ground pepper
50g unsalted butter
4 slices of good quality bread, freshly
* toasted and buttered, to serve*

A day in advance, place the black truffle in a sealed container with the eggs – the truffle aroma will penetrate the shells and flavour the eggs.

Warm a serving dish. Whisk the eggs together in a large bowl, seasoning with salt and just a little pepper. Melt the butter in a heavy-based saucepan over a low heat. Pour in the eggs and cook over a very low heat, stirring almost constantly. They will take quite a while to cook over a gentle heat, but will be all the more delicious as a result.

Just before the eggs are ready, transfer them to the warm serving dish; they will continue to cook in the dish. Using a truffle grater, grate the truffle over the eggs. Serve at once, on hot buttered toast.

Fish & Shellfish

THE SPANISH seafood OBSESSION

The Spanish love eating fish and shellfish. Our favourite seafood restaurants in the world are in Spain and we have often asked ourselves why the seafood in Spain is so much better than it is in this country. We originally thought it was due to the vast coastline and wonderful local species, such as anchovies, squid, San Luca prawns, sardines, tuna and red mullet. A lot of the seafood eaten in Spain is caught locally and of superb quality, but amazingly over half of it is imported from all over the world. It is particularly astonishing that you can often buy fresher English lobsters, crab, cod, Dover Sole, etc., in Spain than you can in the UK.

There are a number of reasons for this. Firstly, the Spanish eat over double the European average of seafood per annum, a huge 31kg per person. Three-quarters of this is cooked and eaten at home, so the Spanish are totally familiar with buying and cooking fish. They certainly know what is fresh and what isn't – they wouldn't touch most of the seafood sold for home cooking in this country with a barge pole! The discerning Spanish public ensures that standards are kept high.

Secondly, the seafood distribution network in Spain is, for the most part, controlled by the state. This has enabled super-efficient transport networks between the ports and cities. Visit the wholesale fish market in San Luca de Barrameda, close to Cadiz, and you will see the day boats pull up alongside the auction house and unload their catch on to the jetty. You can often witness it being auctioned within 10 minutes of unloading, then rushed into waiting refrigerated vans to be dispatched to all parts of Spain.

The markets of Spain are full of weird and wonderful things from beneath the sea. **Percebes** or **goose-necked barnacles** from Galicia look like dinosaur's feet. You steam them briefly before twisting off the leathery outside to reveal little wobbly snorkels that taste as much of the sea as anything we have ever eaten. **Mantis shrimps** from San Luca are another prehistoric looking delicacy, and **sea cucumbers** cooked 'a la plancha' are a real treat. We have also eaten deep-fried **sea anemone**, the outside crisp, the inside creamy like calves' brains. Most of these creatures are best eaten on the day they are caught and are rarely found outside the local area they come from.

At our home in Mallorca we have always enjoyed **fishing for raors** early in the morning from little local rowing boats. These beautiful pink fish have a very short season from August to October and are only found on the sandy bottom of the Mediterranean around the Balearics. Fried in a little oil and sprinkled with salt, they are a great delicacy.

Many of our most **memorable Spanish meals have revolved around seafood**. Most other countries do not have access to the same quality fishmongers and markets that there are in Spain but with a certain degree of selectiveness it possible to replicate the brilliance of the Spanish seafood experience away from Spanish shores.

clams, +
SHERRY
AND ham

We first tasted this dish at our favourite restaurant in the world, the legendary Cal Pep in Barcelona. The trick with this recipe is to keep the pan very, very hot throughout, to ensure that enough of the alcohol from the sherry has evaporated by the time the clams are cooked.

Cut the jamón into little 6mm cubes. Heat a large, heavy-based saucepan until very hot. Throw in the jamón and fry, stirring, for 1 minute. Add the onion and garlic and cook for another minute, stirring constantly.

Add the clams and the sherry, cover with a tight-fitting lid and cook over a high heat for 2 minutes or until the shells have opened. Discard any that stay closed.

Scatter the chopped parsley over the clams, then divide between warm bowls and serve, with good bread for mopping up the juices.

Serves 4 as a starter

50g jamón lardons
½ onion, peeled and finely chopped
2 garlic cloves, peeled and finely chopped
400g fresh clams, cleaned
125ml Fino or Manzanilla sherry
small handful of flat leaf parsley, chopped

We love clams cooked this way, as they seem to convey all the flavours of the sea. This is a really good moment to use your best extra virgin olive oil, as the flavour marries perfectly with the clams.

clams
A LA PLANCHA

Serves 4 as a starter

2–3 tbsp light olive oil
400g fresh clams, cleaned
sea salt and freshly ground pepper
juice of ½ lemon
finest extra virgin olive oil, to drizzle

Heat a little light olive oil on your plancha (see pages 76–7) or in a heavy-based frying pan until just smoking. Throw in the clams and season with salt and pepper. Cook for a couple of minutes, tossing the clams until they open. Discard any that remain closed.

Put the clams, with any cooking juices, into a warm serving dish and squeeze over the lemon juice. Drizzle generously with your finest extra virgin olive oil and serve at once.

mussels VINAIGRETTE

This is a delicious way to eat mussels, particularly during the summer. The recipe is very straightforward and relies simply on good quality fresh mussels, excellent olive oil and sherry vinegar. At Fino, we have recently started buying rope-grown, deep-water mussels from Dorset and have never tasted better.

Heat a large, heavy-based frying pan (with a tight-fitting lid) over a high heat. When the pan is hot and almost smoking, add the mussels with the water and cover with the lid. Cook for about 2 minutes until the mussels have opened. Discard any that remain closed.

Add the extra virgin olive oil, sherry vinegar and herbs. Season with salt and pepper and toss well. Serve immediately, in warm bowls.

Serves 4 as a starter or light meal

1kg fresh mussels, cleaned
25ml water
25ml extra virgin olive oil
1 tbsp sherry vinegar
small handful of flat leaf parsley,
* roughly chopped*
few tiny thyme sprigs
sea salt and freshly ground pepper

The Spanish are keen cockle eaters and so are we. At our house in Mallorca, we often eat canned cockles with lemon juice and a dash of Tabasco as we sip cocktails and watch the sun set slowly over the Mediterranean. This recipe, however, calls for fresh cockles. Feel free to substitute clams if you wish.

cockles IN A SPICY tomato SAUCE

Serves 4 as a starter

1½ tbsp light olive oil
½ onion, peeled and finely chopped
1 chilli (preferably guindilla), deseeded
* and chopped*
2 garlic cloves, peeled and crushed
1 tbsp tomato purée
400g can peeled plum tomatoes
sea salt and freshly ground pepper
400g fresh cockles, cleaned
handful of flat leaf parsley, chopped

Heat the olive oil in large saucepan (with a tight-fitting lid) and fry the onion over a medium heat for 5 minutes. Add the chilli and garlic and fry for another 5 minutes.

Stir in the tomato purée and cook for 2 minutes, then add the canned tomatoes. Bring to the boil, then lower the heat and simmer gently for 35 minutes. Season with salt and pepper to taste.

Add the cockles, cover and cook over a medium heat for 5 minutes or until the shells open. Discard any that remain closed. Add the chopped parsley and serve at once, in warm bowls.

tiger PRAWNS
+ WITH ALIOLI

Like any other shellfish or fish, prawns are only worth buying if they are very fresh and in perfect condition. Look for firm prawns with their feelers and legs intact (these are the first bits to deteriorate). They should smell of the sea (not fishy) and have a healthy translucence about them.

For the accompanying alioli, we like to use a pungent green olive oil here, but for a milder flavour you can use a light olive oil or half virgin olive oil and half groundnut oil. Make the alioli more or less garlicky, depending on whether or not you are planning to kiss anyone that day!

Serves 4 as a starter (or 8 as a tapa)

12–16 large raw prawns
  (2 or 3 per person)
light olive oil for frying
1 garlic clove, peeled and chopped
chopped flat leaf parsley, to serve

for the alioli
1 free-range egg yolk
2–4 garlic cloves, peeled and very
  finely chopped
sea salt and freshly ground pepper
100ml olive oil

First make the alioli. In a bowl, whisk the egg yolk with the garlic and a pinch of salt. Then whisk in the olive oil, drop by drop to begin with, then in a steady stream, until it is all emulsified and you have a thick, garlicky mayonnaise (see note). Season with salt and pepper to taste; set aside.

Wipe the prawns with some kitchen paper to dry them thoroughly. Heat a thin layer of light olive oil in a heavy-based frying pan and add the garlic. Fry the prawns, in batches if necessary, for 3–5 minutes on each side, seasoning with salt and pepper as you go. (Alternatively, you can simply cook them in a large saucepan of heavily salted boiling water for 5 minutes, then drain.)

Serve the prawns scattered with chopped parsley and accompanied by the alioli and some good bread.

note If you mess up and the alioli splits, don't panic. Just break another egg yolk into a clean bowl and slowly whisk in the split mixture. Magically, it will re-combine.

BABY octopus SALAD

This is a great summer dish and can be kept in the fridge for a few days. If you can't track down baby octopus, then a frozen adult octopus also works very well. Just allow an extra 30 minutes' cooking and after draining, cut off the head and slice the tentacles into 2cm rounds.

In a large saucepan, heat plenty of heavily salted water (as salty as the sea) until boiling. Add the octopus, bay leaf and one of the onions, studded with the cloves. Bring back to the boil, then lower the heat to a gentle simmer and cook for 15 minutes or until the octopus is tender. Drain and reserve the octopus, discarding the onion and bay leaf.

Dice the other onion and place in a bowl (large enough to hold all the ingredients). Halve, core, deseed and dice the peppers, then add to the bowl with the fennel and garlic. Add the octopus, sherry vinegar, lemon juice and extra virgin olive oil. Season with salt and pepper to taste. Cover the bowl and place in the fridge for 1 hour.

Just before serving, cut the bread into small cubes. Heat a thin film of light olive oil in a frying pan and fry the bread cubes, turning until crisp and evenly golden. Drain on kitchen paper.

Pile the octopus salad on to individual plates and scatter with the croûtons. Serve straight away.

Serves 4 as a starter (or 8 as a tapa)

1kg baby octopus
sea salt and freshly ground pepper
1 bay leaf
2 onions, peeled
2 cloves
1 red pepper
1 green pepper
½ fennel bulb, trimmed and diced
1 garlic clove, peeled and finely
  chopped
2 tsp sherry vinegar
juice of ½ lemon
75ml extra virgin olive oil
2 slices of good bread, crusts removed
light olive oil for frying

+ COD carpaccio

Here, you need extremely fresh cod and a very sharp knife to slice it finely. As you slice the fish, re-sharpen your knife every 10 slices or so.

Serves 4 as a starter

400g cod fillet, with skin
extra virgin olive oil, to drizzle
juice of ½ lime
sea salt and freshly ground pepper
2 tsp finely chopped capers
¼ red pepper, very finely diced
¼ green pepper, very finely diced
¼ onion, peeled and very finely diced
oregano or torn flat leaf parsley leaves
  (optional)

Lay 4 pieces of cling film, each slightly bigger than your serving plates, on a work surface. Place the cod, skin side down, on a board and slice it horizontally into wafer-thin pieces, about 4cm square. Carefully place the cod slices on the pieces of cling film, overlapping them slightly.

Cover each serving with another piece of cling film, then with the palm of your hand, carefully press down to flatten the cod until you have very fine slices. Refrigerate for 1 hour.

Carefully remove the upper layer of cling film and invert the cod on to serving plates. Remove the other piece of cling film. Drizzle extra virgin olive oil and lime juice all over the cod and season with salt and pepper to taste. Sprinkle with the capers, peppers, onion, and herbs if using. Serve at once.

SEARED tuna +

Seared tuna seems to have such a healthy aura about it, we could eat it almost every day of the week. With this recipe, the tuna is served nearly raw, so it must be very fresh. You also want a really good cut. The best part of the loin is completely smooth, without any flaky bits or sinews, and it will slice beautifully.

Serves 4 as a starter

500g piece of tuna loin (sushi grade)
cracked black pepper
¾ cucumber
1 spring onion, trimmed and chopped
2 chives, finely chopped
2 tsp grainy Dijon mustard
juice of ½ lemon
1 tsp thin honey
sea salt and freshly ground pepper
finest extra virgin olive oil, to drizzle

Pat the tuna dry with kitchen paper, then roll in plenty of cracked black pepper to coat all over. Heat a heavy-based frying pan or plancha (see pages 76–7) until it is very, very hot. Sear the tuna in the very hot pan for about 20–30 seconds on all sides. Remove from the pan and set aside.

Peel the cucumber, halve lengthways and scoop out the seeds, then cut the flesh into 5mm dice. Put into a bowl with the spring onion and chives. Mix the mustard with the lemon juice, honey and some seasoning. Pour over the cucumber mixture and toss well.

Using a razor-sharp carving knife, finely slice the tuna into 5mm thin rounds. You should get 16 slices. Arrange the tuna slices on individual plates, seasoning with salt and drizzling with a little extra virgin olive oil. Serve the dressed cucumber on the side.

LA plancha

La plancha is commonly used as a cooking medium for a myriad of dishes all over Spain. In essence, it is a flat griddle or heavy metal plate that can be maintained at an even temperature. The brilliance of the plancha is two-fold. Firstly, the even temperature prevents food from either sticking or burning. Secondly, the flat surface enables whatever you are cooking to caramelise evenly, rather than just where it hits the ridges on a griddle for example. A

ridged griddle works well for chops, etc., as the rendered fat can run off between the ridges, but with lean foods, such as seafood, mushrooms and lean meat, the plancha really comes into its own.

Cooking 'a la plancha' is easy. You simply lightly oil your plancha, heat it to the required temperature, carefully dry whatever you are cooking with kitchen paper…and you are away! The ideal temperature for cooking most things on the plancha is 180°C. Once you have mastered the technique, the possibilities for simple, delicious food are endless. At Fino, we cook whole fish, fish fillets, lobster, squid, scallops, mussels, clams, mushrooms, spring onions, aubergines, asparagus, eggs, fillet steak, veal cutlets – even foie gras – on our plancha.

You can buy an excellent electric plancha from some kitchen equipment suppliers, but it will set you back a few hundred pounds. The next possibility is the heavy metal plancha that is designed to sit over a gas hob. This works quite well, but is prone to hot spots. Often domestic gas hobs have adjacent burners of different sizes, which makes it difficult, though not impossible, to obtain the vital even heat on all parts of the plancha.

If you own an Aga, you have **the perfect plancha built into the range**. Cooking directly on the hot hob of the Aga is effectively cooking 'a la plancha' and, as it burns all the grease off, it is self-cleaning as well.

A good quality, large, heavy-based frying pan is a simple solution if you have none of the aforementioned items of equipment in your kitchen. All you need to do is to **maintain the pan at an even heat**. If you oil the pan with light olive oil, then 180°C is about right. This is the temperature at which light olive oil will just begin to smoke a little. If the pan is not smoking at all, it is too cold; if it is smoking a lot, it is too hot. When you start cooking, the contents of your pan should sizzle fairly vigorously, but again there shouldn't be too much smoke.

Our advice is to **heat the pan until it is about 20°C hotter than you need it**, as the temperature will drop by about this amount when you add the food, and you can then lower the heat a little to maintain it there. If you want to be more accurate and do this scientifically, you can buy a special thermometer that fires an infra-red beam at any surface and displays its temperature. In any case, you will soon learn what sort of flame you need to maintain a steady cooking temperature.

As with all aspects of cooking, **practise makes perfect**, but we would urge you to master the skill of cooking 'a la plancha' as it is at the root of Spanish cooking.

lobster A LA + PLANCHA

First combine all the ingredients for the dressing in a bowl; set aside.

To kill the lobster instantly, hold it firmly on a board and thrust the point of a strong knife into the cross on the head and down through the body to halve it lengthways. Discard the sac near the head and the dark intestinal thread. Snap the claws off and crack them slightly with a mallet. Save the edible dark meat, and coral if there is any.

Lightly oil the plancha (see pages 76–7) and heat until slightly smoking. Add the claws and cook for 5 minutes on each side. After 2 minutes, put the lobster halves, shell side down, on the plancha and cook for 6 minutes. Cook the reserved dark meat (and coral if any) directly on a well-oiled part of the plancha for a minute or two. Remove and cool slightly, then mix into the dressing. Turn the lobster over and cook for another 2–3 minutes.

Serve the lobster at once, drizzled with the dressing.

Serves 2

1 live lobster, about 1kg
olive oil for cooking

for the dressing
5 cherry tomatoes, finely chopped
$\frac{1}{2}$ red chilli, deseeded and finely chopped
10 basil leaves, finely sliced
50ml extra virgin olive oil
juice of $\frac{1}{2}$ lemon
sea salt and freshly ground pepper

squid + A LA PLANCHA

Serves 4

500g squid, cleaned (see page 22)
3 tbsp good quality virgin olive oil
1 red chilli (medium heat), deseeded and finely chopped
2 tsp finely chopped flat leaf parsley
1 garlic clove, peeled and finely diced
juice of $\frac{1}{2}$ lemon
sea salt and freshly ground pepper

Using a sharp knife, cut open the squid pouches and lightly score them in a criss-cross fashion. Pat the squid pouches and tentacles dry with kitchen paper and keep to one side.

Heat the olive oil on your plancha or in a large, heavy-based frying pan over a high heat. Add the squid and cook, without moving, for 1$\frac{1}{2}$ minutes. Turn the squid over and cook for another minute.

Transfer the squid to a warm plate and add the chilli, parsley, garlic and lemon juice. Season to taste and serve immediately.

Toasted almonds and peppery watercress in a sherry vinegar dressing are the perfect match for pan-fried sea bass fillets. Buy wild rather than farmed sea bass, if possible, as the flavour and texture are far superior. Also farmed sea bass are rarely allowed to reach a decent size, so their fillets are usually too thin and tend to dry out before the skin crisps nicely.

✚ sea bass WITH WATERCRESS

Serves 4

100g blanched almonds
4 sea bass fillets, about 150g each
sea salt and freshly ground pepper
olive oil for cooking
1 large bunch of watercress, trimmed

for the dressing

3 tbsp extra virgin olive oil
1½ tbsp Jerez sherry vinegar
1½ tbsp thin honey
1 shallot, peeled and finely chopped

Preheat the oven to 180°C/Gas 4. Spread out the almonds on a baking tray and toast them in the oven for about 10 minutes, turning once or twice until nicely browned and taking care not to let any burn. Cool sightly, then break up the almonds with a rolling pin and set aside.

Pat the sea bass fillets thoroughly dry with kitchen paper – this prevents them from sticking in the pan and ensures that the skin will crisp nicely. Using a very sharp knife, make 2 or 3 shallow cuts in the skin of each fillet, stopping 1cm before you reach the other side. Season the skin side with salt. Oil your plancha or a large, heavy-based frying pan – you need enough olive oil to thinly coat the bottom. Place over a high heat until the oil is just beginning to smoke.

Put the sea bass fillets, skin side down, on the plancha or in the pan. Season the up side with a little salt. Cook over a high heat for about 3 minutes until the fillets begin to caramelise and brown at the edges. Carefully turn the fillets over and cook for a further 2 minutes, then remove from the plancha or pan and leave to rest in a warm place for 5 minutes.

Meanwhile, for the dressing, whisk the ingredients together in a bowl, seasoning to taste with salt and pepper. In a large bowl, toss the watercress with the dressing.

Divide the salad between warm plates and place the sea bass fillets on top. Scatter the almonds over and spoon on any remaining dressing. Serve immediately.

hake
WITH
salsa VERDE

We acquired the recipe for this Basque speciality from Nieves, our wonderful sous chef at Fino, who comes from San Turce in Bilbao. Generally, the English don't share the Spanish enthusiasm for hake, which is a shame as a good hake is as tasty to eat as any other fish.

First make the salsa verde. Pour the extra virgin olive oil into a blender and start to blitz, gradually adding the spinach, parsley, mint and oregano leaves through the feeder funnel. Add the capers and mustard and blend to a fine purée. Finally add the lemon juice and season with salt and pepper to taste. Set aside.

To cook the hake, carefully pat the steaks dry with kitchen paper. Heat a thin film of olive oil in a large, heavy-based frying pan over a high heat until it just starts to smoke. Carefully place the hake steaks in the pan and reduce the heat to medium. Fry for 4–5 minutes on each side, seasoning lightly with salt. Try to maintain an even temperature in the pan – the oil should be sizzling, but not burning. Equally if the pan is not sizzling happily and smoking just a little, then the temperature will be too low and the fish is liable to stick.

Remove the hake from the pan and place on a warm platter. Leave to rest in a warm place for 2 minutes before serving, with the salsa verde.

Serves 6

6 hake medallions, each 5–6cm thick
olive oil for cooking

for the salsa verde
150ml extra virgin olive oil
40g baby spinach leaves
30g flat leaf parsley, stalks removed
10g mint sprigs, stalks removed
1 oregano sprig, leaves stripped
20g capers, drained
2 tsp Dijon mustard
juice of ½ lemon
sea salt and freshly ground pepper

cod BILBAINA

The success of this recipe really depends upon using the freshest of fish. If you are concerned as to whether your cod hails from sustainable stocks, then consider using hake or turbot – both great substitutes. Ask your fishmonger for equal-sized, thick fillets, to ensure they all take the same time to cook and remain succulent. The flavour of the sherry vinegar combined with the tomatoes gives the sauce a special character. Needless to say, the riper and sweeter the tomatoes, the better the end result.

Serves 4

4 cod fillets, about 200g each and
* 4cm thick*
1 tbsp light olive oil
sea salt and freshly ground pepper

for the tomato sauce

12 small midi plum tomatoes or
* cherry tomatoes*
4 garlic cloves, peeled
2 tbsp light olive oil
2 bay leaves
2 tbsp Fino or Manzanilla sherry
2 tbsp sherry vinegar

First make the tomato sauce. Remove the stalk ends of the tomatoes, then cut them in half lengthways. Cut the garlic lengthways into thin slices. Place a large frying pan over a medium heat and add the olive oil. Add the tomato halves with the garlic slices and bay leaves and cook for 3–4 minutes or until soft. Add the sherry and sherry vinegar, stirring to deglaze the pan, and allow to bubble and reduce for 2 minutes. Season with salt and pepper to taste and set aside.

Preheat the oven to 180°C/Gas 4. Pat the cod fillets dry with kitchen paper. Heat a large ovenproof frying pan over a medium-high heat and add the olive oil. Put the cod pieces in the pan, skin side down, and fry for 4 minutes. Transfer the pan to the oven (leaving the cod skin side down) and cook for a further 4 minutes. In the meantime, reheat the tomato sauce if necessary.

Using a metal spatula, carefully lift the fish on to warm plates and season with salt and pepper. Spoon the tomato sauce alongside and serve at once.

note If you do not own an ovenproof frying pan, use a heavy-based frying pan and transfer the fish to an oiled, preheated baking tray before you put it into the oven.

sea bream
BAKED IN salt

We are obsessed with cooking fish on the plancha. The only other method that really inspires us is baking in salt. The amazing smell when you crack into the crust and release the aromas of the baked fish is fantastic. The salt also seals in all the juices resulting in deliciously juicy flesh. The other great thing about baking in salt is that you cannot check the progress of the fish as you are cooking. This ensures a nail-biting finale when you crack the crust and discover if the cooking time was right and whether your oven was really at the right temperature! The Spanish eat a lot of farmed sea bream but we would advise making the effort to source the wild variety.

Serves 2

2kg salt
2 free-range egg whites
2 sea bream (doradas), about
  400–500g each, cleaned
2 bay leaves
2 thyme sprigs
2 garlic cloves, peeled
2 lemon slices
freshly ground pepper

Preheat the oven to 180°C/Gas 4. In a large bowl, mix the salt with the egg whites. Carefully dry the fish with kitchen paper. Stuff the cavities with the bay leaves, thyme sprigs, garlic cloves and lemon slices, seasoning with a little pepper.

On a large roasting tray, make two salt bases, about 1.5cm thick, each slightly larger than the fish. Place the fish on the salt bases and cover them with a layer of salt, at least 1cm thick. If you are feeling artistic, you can mould the salt into the shape of a fish and mark on an eye, mouth, scales and fins.

Bake the fish in the oven for 17 minutes. Remove from the oven and leave to stand at room temperature for 5 minutes. Then crack open the salt crust and serve on individual platters. To eat, carefully remove the salt and skin from the top side of the fish and eat that side first. Then lift off the head and bone and eat the bottom half, again discarding the skin.

crab
+ A LA
VASCA

This Basque dish is wonderful served hot, warm or cold with a large green salad and a loaf of crusty sourdough. Try to find a large crab as opposed to two smaller ones, as there is much less work in the picking.

To cook a live crab, place in a large saucepan of water and bring to the boil. Add a bay leaf and ½ onion and cook for 20–25 minutes. Remove the crab from the water and allow to cool.

To prepare the crab, remove the claws and legs and set aside. Lay the crab on its back and twist off the tail flap then, holding the shell firmly, push up the body section until you can lift it out. Remove and discard the dead man's fingers. Carefully pick out all the white and brown meat from the crab and keep to one side. Crack open the large claws, take out all the meat and add it to the rest of the crab.

Heat the olive oil in a large frying pan over a medium heat and add the leek, chilli, shallot and garlic with the other bay leaf. Fry, stirring occasionally, for 10 minutes or until softened. Add the white and brown crab meat with the canned tomatoes and cook gently for 5 minutes. Add the sherry and brandy, and let bubble to reduce and evaporate the alcohol for 5–6 minutes.

Scatter chopped parsley over the crab and serve with plenty of bread.

Serves 4

1 fresh large, crab, about 1.2kg
   (preferably live)
2 bay leaves
½ onion, peeled
3 tbsp light olive oil
1 leek, trimmed and finely chopped
1 red chilli, deseeded and finely
   chopped
1 shallot, peeled and finely chopped
1 garlic clove, peeled and finely
   chopped
400g can chopped tomatoes
100ml Manzanilla or Fino sherry
3 tbsp brandy
2–3 tbsp finely chopped flat leaf
   parsley

CALDERETA
+ DE
langosta

We have fond memories of eating this fine lobster stew
on the beach in Formentera at a party for our dear
friend Thomas Davies. It kept body and soul together,
even if the rest of the weekend is something of a blur!
If you cannot find Mediterranean spiny lobsters,
then their Scottish cousins, which are also known
as rock lobsters, will do adequately.

To prepare the lobsters, first kill them (following the instructions on page 79), unless of course your fishmonger has done this for you. Break off the claws and legs, then twist off the heads from the lobsters and remove the stomach sac and gills. Chop each head into 4 pieces; reserve. Remove the meat from the body shell and discard the dark intestinal vein. Slice the meat into 3cm medallions; set aside.

Heat the olive oil in a large, heavy-based pan or flameproof casserole and fry the onions, garlic, carrots and celery for 5 minutes. Add the lobster heads and continue to fry until they are golden brown.

Add the tomato purée, tomatoes, thyme, bay leaf, oregano and parsley and cook for 10 minutes. Add the brandy and carefully ignite to burn off the alcohol. Add the white wine and water, bring to the boil and then lower the heat. Simmer for about 20 minutes.

Add the lobster medallions to the pan and cook over a low heat for 5 minutes. In the meantime, heat a thin film of olive oil in a frying pan and fry the bread slices until nicely browned on both sides. Drain on kitchen paper and rub with the cut garlic clove.

Place a slice of fried bread in each warm serving bowl and ladle the lobster stew on top. Scatter over a little chopped parsley and serve at once, with lemon wedges on the side.

Serves 4

2 live spiny lobsters, about 1.5kg each
2 tbsp light olive oil
2 onions, peeled and diced
10 garlic cloves, peeled and finely
  chopped
3 carrots, peeled and diced
2 celery sticks, diced
2 tsp tomato purée
10 small tomatoes, skinned,
  deseeded and diced
1 thyme sprig
1 bay leaf
1 small oregano sprig
small handful of chopped flat leaf
  parsley
50ml brandy
75ml white wine
500ml water

for the fried garlic bread
light olive oil
4 slices of good quality rustic bread
1 garlic clove (unpeeled), cut

to serve
handful of chopped parsley
lemon wedges

FRIT marinér ✚

The bold flavours in this rustic dish make it a firm favourite.
We have fond memories of eating it at our local beach bar on
the northwest coast of Mallorca. There is something about
emerging from the sea and devouring a cold beer and a large
plate of 'frit' before finding a shady spot for a quiet snooze.
Leave the tail shells on the prawns if you prefer to eat them
with your fingers.

Serves 6 (or 12 as a starter)

500g medium raw prawns
500g squid, cleaned (see page 22)
125ml olive oil
2 onions, peeled and diced
2 potatoes, peeled and diced
1 aubergine, trimmed and diced
1 fennel bulb, trimmed and diced
2 large red peppers, cored, deseeded
  and diced
5 garlic cloves, peeled and finely sliced
1 chilli, deseeded and finely diced
sea salt and freshly ground pepper
large handful of flat leaf parsley,
  chopped
lemon wedges, to serve

Shell and devein the prawns. Slice the squid pouches into 1cm rings.
In a heavy-based frying pan or paella pan (large enough to hold all the
ingredients), heat the olive oil until smoking, then fry the squid and
prawns for 2–3 minutes until just cooked. Remove with a slotted spoon
and set aside.

Add the onions, potatoes, aubergine, fennel, peppers, garlic and chilli
to the pan. Fry over a medium-low heat, gently stirring occasionally, until
golden brown and caramelised, about 45 minutes – 1 hour. During
cooking, season the vegetables well with salt and pepper. They take quite
a lot of seasoning, so keep tasting and adjust as necessary.

Add the squid and prawns to the vegetables and cook for 2 minutes.
Throw in the chopped parsley and serve with lemon wedges and some
good rustic bread.

This Catalan fish soup is served all over the region, its contents varying according to the fish and shellfish available in the locality at the time. Meaning 'operetta', sarsuela is a richly varied combination, but it is the freshness of the ingredients that is of prime importance, rather than the actual varieties of seafood included. Feel free to substitute any of the fish or shellfish listed below, but do make sure you use a rockfish for the soup. Other additions might include razor clams, cockles, lobster or monkfish. Ideally, you need at least three or four kinds of shellfish and at least two different fish... have some fun and use your imagination.

sarsuela

Serves 6

for the soup base

1 tbsp olive oil
1 gurnard or other rockfish, about 1kg,
  or 2 smaller fish, 500g each, cleaned
grated zest of 1 orange
3 onions, peeled and roughly chopped
1kg tomatoes, roughly chopped
1 celery stick, roughly chopped
4 carrots, peeled and roughly chopped
1 head of garlic, sliced in half
  horizontally
2 tbsp tomato purée
300ml Fino or Manzanilla sherry
200ml dry anis or Pernod
small pinch of saffron threads
3 litres water

for the sarsuela

olive oil for frying
6 large raw prawns, cleaned
6 raw langoustines (preferably live)
6 hake medallions, about 750g in total
6 small whole red mullet, cleaned, or
  6 medium red mullet fillets
250g squid, cleaned (see page 22)
  and cut into 1cm rings
30 fresh clams or small mussels
sea salt and freshly ground pepper
2 onions, peeled and finely diced
2 fennel bulbs, finely diced
lemon juice, to taste

to serve

chopped flat leaf parsley
alioli (see page 70)

To make the soup base, heat the olive oil in a heavy-based casserole. Add the whole fish with the orange zest and fry, mashing the fish down with the back of a spoon, until deep brown. Add the onions, tomatoes, celery, carrots and garlic and continue to cook over a medium heat for 20 minutes. Add the tomato purée and cook for a further 10 minutes.

Add the sherry and anis. Bring to the boil and then, off the heat, carefully ignite to burn off all the alcohol. Return to the heat, add the saffron and water and bring to the boil. Lower the heat to a simmer and cook for 40–50 minutes, skimming off any impurities that rise to the surface from time to time. Strain the contents of the casserole twice through a fine sieve and reserve the liquid, discarding the residue.

For the sarsuela, in a large, heavy-based casserole (big enough to hold all the ingredients), heat a 5mm depth of olive oil until very hot but not smoking. Quickly and carefully fry all the fish and seafood except the clams (or mussels), in batches if necessary, for about 2 minutes on each side, seasoning with salt and pepper as you go. Carefully remove from the pan and set aside.

Gently fry the onions and fennel in the casserole, adding a little more oil if necessary, for 5 minutes. Add the soup base and bring to the boil, scraping up the sediment from the bottom of the casserole. As soon as the liquid comes to the boil, lower the heat and simmer gently for about 10 minutes. Add all the pre-fried seafood and cook for 5 minutes.

Add the clams (or mussels) and simmer for a further 5 minutes or until all the seafood is cooked. Season with salt and pepper and add a generous squeeze of lemon juice to taste.

Scatter chopped parsley over the Sarsuela and serve at once, with alioli and plenty of good bread.

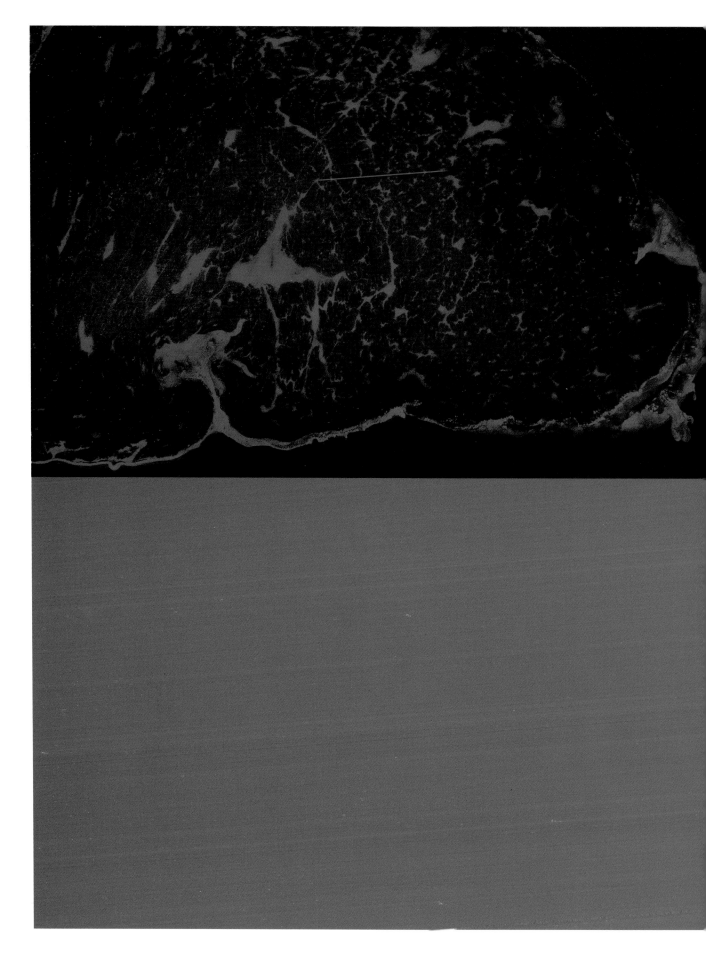

MARINATED GRILLED quail

Quail is very popular in Spain and it is cooked in many different ways. Here the small birds are marinated with chilli, spices and honey to enhance their flavour. The quails are spatchcocked (split and flattened) so they can be griddled quickly and evenly. Your butcher will probably do this if you ask, otherwise you can easily do it yourself. In the summer, the quail can be cooked on the barbecue, but you will need to take care to avoid scorching the breast meat as the honey caramelises quickly.

Serves 4

4 free-range quails, preferably ready-
  spatchcocked
4 white peppercorns
2 cloves
1 star anise
2 tbsp thin honey
splash of sherry vinegar
few thyme sprigs
½ red chilli, deseeded and chopped

If the quails are not already spatchcocked, you will need to do this yourself. Using a sharp knife or poultry shears, cut down one side of the backbone along the length of the quail. Cut down the other side of the backbone and then remove it. Open out the bird and clean the inside, removing any offal. Cut the ends of the ribcage away, leaving a neatly trimmed bird. With the skin side uppermost, press down on the breastbone to flatten the bird. Push two fine wooden skewers through each quail, crosswise from opposite wings to legs to hold them flat.

Put the quail in a large bowl and add the peppercorns, cloves, star anise, honey, sherry vinegar, thyme and chilli. Toss well to mix and leave to marinate in the fridge for 24 hours. Take out of the fridge about an hour before cooking to bring the quail to room temperature.

Place a griddle pan over a high heat until almost smoking. Remove the quail from the marinade and cook them on the hot griddle for about 2 minutes on each side, basting with the marinade. Transfer to a warm plate and leave the quail to rest in a warm place for 2 minutes. Drizzle the cooking juices over the quail and serve immediately.

ROAST. partridge WITH lentils +

In Spain, you will come across partridge in various forms ~ even pickled and canned ~ but as far as we are concerned the best way to treat this game bird is to roast it very simply. Grey-legged partridges have the finest flavour, if you can find them. Don't fall into the trap of being overly organised and browning your birds well ahead of roasting, they need to be hot when they enter the oven.

Serves 4

*4 partridges, cleaned (giblets reserved
  if available)*
handful of thyme sprigs
2 tbsp olive oil
2 slices of streaky bacon, chopped
1 onion, peeled and diced
1 carrot, peeled and diced
1 celery stick, diced
3 garlic cloves, peeled and crushed
150g Puy lentils
1 bay leaf
400ml water
50g butter
sea salt and freshly ground pepper
250ml Fino or Manzanilla sherry

Preheat the oven to 200°C/Gas 6. If you have the partridge giblets, chop the liver and heart; set aside. Carefully dry the partridges inside and out with kitchen paper, then stuff a few thyme sprigs into the cavities.

Heat the olive oil in a saucepan and fry the bacon, onion, carrot, celery and garlic in the olive oil, together with the chopped offal if using, until soft and translucent. Add the lentils, bay leaf, 1 thyme sprig and the water. Bring to the boil, then reduce the heat and simmer for 40 minutes or until the lentils are tender, covering the pan if they appear to be dry.

Heat the butter in a large, heavy-based, ovenproof frying pan until sizzling. Brown the partridges on all sides, seasoning with salt and pepper as you go and being careful not to burn the butter.

Sit the partridges breast side up and put the pan into the hot oven. Roast for 10 minutes. (If your pan isn't ovenproof, simply transfer the partridges to an oiled, preheated roasting pan.)

Remove from the oven, cover with foil and leave to rest in a warm place for 10 minutes, then lift the partridges on to a warmed platter, saving the juices in the pan. Re-cover the birds with the foil and return to their resting place while you finish the lentils.

Reheat the juices in the pan, then add the sherry to deglaze, scraping up all the caramelised bits from the bottom. Add the lentils and cook for 2 minutes. Season and serve with the roasted partridges.

slow-COOKED rabbit

Rabbit can often be disappointingly dry, though this dish is anything but, which is why it works so well. The large quantity of vegetables and chopped tomatoes make a robust sauce that keeps the rabbit from drying out as it cooks. For this recipe, ask your butcher for a farmed rabbit and get him to joint it into 10 or 12 pieces, unless you prefer to do so at home. First joint the back legs off the rabbit, then the front legs. Trim the flap of skin off either side of the body, then joint into 6 pieces. You can also separate the back legs and thighs if you wish.

Serves 6

4 tbsp light olive oil
1 rabbit, jointed
2 cooking chorizo sausages, cut into 2cm rounds
1 onion, peeled and roughly chopped
3 garlic cloves, peeled and thinly sliced
1 red pepper, cored, deseeded and diced
1 green pepper, cored, deseeded and diced
2 carrots, peeled and diced
2 celery sticks, sliced
1 leek, trimmed and sliced
2 bay leaves
3 thyme sprigs
3 piquillo peppers, cut into strips
1 red chilli, deseeded and finely diced
1 tsp sweet paprika
400g can chopped tomatoes
200ml Fino or Manzanilla sherry
sea salt and freshly ground pepper
2 tbsp chopped flat leaf parsley

Heat the olive oil in a large casserole or deep frying pan over a medium heat. Add the rabbit pieces and chorizo slices and brown for 10 minutes, turning to colour evenly on all sides. Remove the meat from the casserole and set aside.

Add the onion, garlic and red and green peppers to the casserole and cook for 5 minutes. Add the carrots, celery, leek, bay leaves and thyme and cook for a further 5 minutes.

Add the piquillo peppers, diced chilli and paprika and mix well. Return the browned rabbit and chorizo to the casserole, add the tomatoes and sherry and cook for 30 minutes until the rabbit is cooked through. Season with salt and pepper to taste.

Scatter over the chopped parsley and serve immediately, with Olive oil mash (see page 136) and Green beans and shallots (see page 137).

+ chicken WITH red PEPPERS

This is a very simple, rustic dish that we have enjoyed for years, as it is one that our mother cooks for family meals. The secret here is to make sure your heat isn't too high, otherwise the chicken will scorch on the outside before it is cooked in the middle. The peppers and chicken make their own tasty pan juices, but if you want a little more sauce, deglaze the pan with a little sherry or white wine after you have removed the chicken (but not the peppers). Neither of us would ever consider using a chicken that was not free- range...hopefully neither will you!

Joint the chicken into 8 pieces. First remove the thighs and legs, then the wings (at an angle with some breast meat attached), then the 2 breasts. Separate the thighs from the legs to give you 8 pieces. Halve the red peppers, remove the core and seeds, then cut into broad strips.

In a large, heavy-based frying pan (big enough to hold all the chicken easily), heat the olive oil until just smoking. Add the chicken pieces and fry over a medium heat for about 5 minutes, turning to colour well on all sides and seasoning with salt and pepper.

Add the onions, red peppers, garlic, thyme and bay leaves. Cook over a medium heat, turning and stirring occasionally, for 30–45 minutes until the chicken is cooked through. Take off the heat, cover and leave to rest in a warm place for 10 minutes before serving.

Serves 4

1 free-range chicken, about 1.5kg
2 red peppers
2 tbsp olive oil
sea salt and freshly ground pepper
2 onions, peeled and sliced
6 garlic cloves, peeled and chopped
2 thyme sprigs
4 bay leaves

chorizo AND tomato
+ SALAD

This combination of hot, spicy chorizo and cold tomatoes works brilliantly as a warm salad. The only proviso is that your tomatoes and chorizo are both excellent. We like to use the picante or spicy chorizo here, although you could opt for a mild chorizo if you prefer. Flavourful, ripe, juicy tomatoes are essential.

For a light lunch, serve with some crusty bread. Both spicy chorizo and tomatoes are wine killers, but a nice glass of cold Manzanilla or Fino sherry goes perfectly.

Serves 2 as a light meal
(4 as a starter, or 6 as a tapa)

500g small ripe plum tomatoes
2 spring onions, trimmed and finely
  chopped
sea salt and freshly ground pepper
50ml extra virgin olive oil
1 tbsp sherry vinegar
250g picante or other cooking chorizo
  sausage
1 tbsp light olive oil
1–2 tbsp torn flat leaf parsley

Halve the plum tomatoes and put into a bowl. Add the spring onions and season with salt and pepper. Drizzle with the extra virgin olive oil and sherry vinegar and toss to mix. Set aside to marinate for 30 minutes.

Cut the chorizo on the diagonal into chunky 1.5cm slices. Heat the light olive oil in a heavy-based frying pan and gently fry the chorizo slices for 2 minutes on each side. Add 2 or 3 tsp of the oil from the pan to the tomatoes and toss to mix.

Transfer the tomatoes and spring onions to serving plates and pile the hot chorizo slices on top. Spoon the juices from the tomato bowl over the salad, add a grinding of pepper and scatter over some torn parsley leaves to serve.

SPANISH fiestas

Celebrations are so numerous in Spain, you could argue that the country constantly appears to be in the throes of one continuous fiesta. Midweek fiesta days are often bridged to the weekend to create a 'puente' or long weekend off work. We can't think of another country so inclined to endless partying. Each village, town and city celebrates a patron saint's day. This is often the most important fiesta of the year and can last for days or even a week. In addition there may be other fiestas throughout the year, as well as national holidays.

Most religious fiestas in Spain follow a similar format of processions led by local men terrifyingly clad in 'penetentes' or penitent clothing, long robes and tall pointed hats carrying an ornate float on their shoulders through the streets. This can be a solemn and impressive spectacle. Services in churches are attended and families eat and celebrate together, uniting young and old.

The more light-hearted side of the fiesta comes in the form of dancing, eating, drinking and merriment in the streets. Groups of children of various ages play on the church steps while their parents enjoy good food, good wine and time with their friends, not to forget the aged who join in too. Only in Spain have we come across parties that are so inclusive of all age groups.

Whichever fiesta you decide to visit, it is important to respect the traditions and serious side of these events, to pace yourself as you will need stamina, and to make sure you see all that is on offer. Happy Fiestas!

Fiestas well worth a visit...

San Fermin   *6th–14th July*

This famous fiesta takes place in Pamplona in northern Spain. The entertainment centres on the *encierros* (running of the bulls), although there is much more on offer. Predominantly it is the wild youth of Pamplona who run with the bulls, wearing red scarves and armed with rolled up newspapers, though some foolhardy outsiders take part as well. Should you wish to join in the *encierros*, which is highly unadvisable, you need to be wearing running shoes, armed with a rolled newspaper and completely sober!

San Isidro   *1st–31st May*

This fiesta is named after San Isidore, one of Madrid's patron saints. From 2nd May, Madrid celebrates the insurrection that built up into the Spanish War of Independence. The festivities have hardly finished by May 15th, San Isidore's day. Concerts are held in the Plaza Mayor and the Vistillas Park becomes an open-air dance hall. The bull fighting festival runs for almost an entire month at Las Ventas, Madrid's bullring.

Las Fallas de San Jose   *15th–19th March*

In Valencia and surrounding towns, massive wood and papier-mâché monuments (*fallas*) are erected and lavishly decorated. These are intended as scathing attacks on aspects of local and national affairs. There are daily firework displays and the combined smell of gunpowder and paellas cooking over wood fires is overwhelming. The culmination of the fiesta is at midnight on the final night, when the *fallas* are set alight.

La Tomatina   *end of August*

This orgy of tomato throwing in Buñol, east of Valencia, has become a tourist attraction. Lorry loads of overripe tomatoes are dumped in the town for revellers to launch at one another. Everyone ends up covered in tomato pulp.

La Feria de Sevilla   *late April*

This fiesta takes place in the second or third week after Easter in Seville, and on a lesser scale in Cordoba, Granada and Almería. Originally a livestock fair, this has turned into a week-long celebration, held in a purpose built fairground out of the city. It is a great society event, where wealth and fame are flaunted, although anyone can join in. Andalucian horses and women in classical flamenco dress are accompanied by copious amounts of Fino sherry, flamenco music and Sevillana dancing.

Carnival de Cadiz   *3rd–13th February*

This dates back to the time when Cadiz was one of Spain's most important trading ports. There are numerous musical acts with African and Creole influences as well as local songs and traditional flamenco music, plus rock concerts, raucous parades, comedians and children's performances. A huge cacophony of fire crackers takes place each day in Plaza San Juan.

La Procession de los Borachos
Good Friday

Cuenca welcomes orchestral and choral groups to a week-long festival of religious music in the church of San Miguel during the week before Easter. At dawn on Good Friday 'the procession of the drunkards' takes place. Along the route the marchers are heckled by the *turbas* (mob), who are supposed to represent the Jews who scorned Christ as he bore the cross to Calvary. Typically, they are inebriated on the powerful local brew, *resoli*.

Fiesta de los Moros y Christianos
22nd–24th April

This fiesta in Alcoi (50km North of Alicante) celebrates the reconquest of Spain (and eviction of the Moors). Almost the whole town gathers in glittering costumes around a mock castle in the middle of the town for three days in an amazing display of street theatre.

ROAST suckling PIG

There is nothing quite like a whole suckling pig for a special occasion. Most good butchers in this country will obtain one for you, as long as you order it in advance. It isn't difficult to achieve perfectly crisp skin on your suckling pig, provided you allow plenty of time for roasting. At the temperature we use, the skin won't burn and the meat is so succulent that it's unlikely to dry out with overcooking. So, if the pig is not perfectly crisp after 2½ hours, just return it to the oven until it is. If you allow 3 hours to start with and it is crisp half an hour earlier, your pig will happily rest in a warm place until you are ready to eat.

Serves 10–12

1 suckling pig, 5–6kg
2 heads of garlic, separated into
  cloves and peeled
2 shallots, peeled and halved
2 dried red peppers
6 thyme sprigs
5 bay leaves
2 lemons, sliced
a little olive oil
sea salt and freshly ground pepper

Preheat the oven to 180°C/Gas 4. Lay the pig, belly down on a large board with the legs splayed out to the sides. Push down hard on the backbone to open up the ribcage and flatten it down on to the board.

If the pig is too big to fit in one large roasting pan (we usually find it is), cut it in two across the middle, using a sharp, heavy knife. Put the head and shoulder end in one roasting pan and the leg and tail end in another. Pat the meat dry with kitchen paper.

Lift up the pig and scatter the garlic, shallots, dried peppers, thyme, bay leaves and lemon slices underneath it. Rub the skin all over with olive oil, then season well with salt and pepper. Place the roasting pans in the oven and roast for 1 hour. Swap the roasting pans around (to ensure even cooking) and cook for another hour. Transpose the roasting pans again and cook for a further 30 minutes.

Now check to see if the skin is wonderfully crisp and deep brown. If so, transfer to warm platters and set aside to rest in a warm place until ready to carve. If not, return the pig to the oven for 20–30 minutes.

To carve the pig, firstly remove the legs and shoulders and carve the meat from them, taking care that each slice of meat has a portion of crisp skin attached. Then carve the meat from the saddle and the ribs, again keeping the skin attached to the meat. If you are squeamish about the other bits, sprinkle what you have carved with plenty of salt and serve at once. If you are an offal fan, read on!

The pig's head is a great treat. Remove it from the body, then slice it in half lengthways. Inside you will find some delicious brain and tongue. The snout, ears and cheeks all make excellent eating, too. Oh, and of course, don't forget the crispy tail!

leg OF MILK-FED + lamb

Spain has always had an abundance of milk-fed lamb, due to the desire to sell off young lambs while the mother is still milking, in order to use the milk to make cheese. Until recently, this special meat has been difficult to source in this country, but owing to demand and an increase in small ewe's milk cheese producers, it is now less of a foreign delicacy.

A small leg of milk-fed lamb is such a treat. The legs we use at the restaurant are the size specified in the recipe and we have given appropriate timings. You can use larger legs, but you will need to adjust the roasting time accordingly.

Preheat the oven to 180°C/Gas 4. Make 2 incisions, about 6cm long, across the fleshy side of each lamb leg. In each incision, stuff a small sprig of rosemary and 3 slices of garlic. Rub each lamb leg all over with olive oil and season with salt and pepper.

Heat 1 tbsp olive oil in a large roasting pan over a medium heat. Add the lamb legs and brown for 2–3 minutes on each side. Transfer to the oven and roast the lamb for 25 minutes, basting occasionally with the pan juices.

Check that the meat is cooked by inserting a skewer into the thickest part (see below). When the lamb is ready, cover loosely with foil and leave to rest in a warm place for 15–20 minutes. Carve the meat and serve, with Tumbet (see page 143).

note One of the best ways of testing whether the meat is ready is to insert a skewer or knife into the middle of the thickest part. Leave the implement there for 30 seconds, then remove and touch the very tip of the skewer lightly on your top lip.

If it feels warm, the meat will be cooked medium-rare and is ready. If it is cold, the meat is raw in the middle and you need to roast the joints for longer. If the tip is hot, the meat will be well done.

Serves 4

2 small legs of lamb, 700–800g
  each, from a milk-fed lamb
4 rosemary sprigs
2 garlic cloves, peeled and thinly
  sliced
2–3 tbsp light olive oil
sea salt and freshly ground pepper

CRISP
pork BELLY

This is one of our most popular dishes at Fino and it is easy to see why. The crisp crackling combined with the succulent meat is really superb. Please make the effort to seek out good quality pork.

Commercial farmers get pigs from birth to slaughter weight in about 18 weeks by feeding them a cocktail of growth supplements and keeping them indoors, so they take little exercise. A naturally reared pig that lives outside will take about 40 weeks to reach the same weight. It doesn't take a genius to work out which animal will have had a better quality of life, and be more flavoursome to eat. Remember, a happy pig is a delicious pig...

When buying the pork belly, get the butcher to remove the ribs and score the skin for you.

To prepare the pork belly, rub plenty of sea salt into the skin side and set aside for 1 hour.

Preheat the oven to 220°C/Gas 7. Using kitchen paper or a clean tea-towel, rub off the salt and dry the skin well. Place the pork belly, skin side down, in a lightly oiled roasting pan. Season the up side with salt and pepper, then sprinkle with the cumin seeds and thyme leaves.

Roast in the oven for 30 minutes, then reduce the setting to 190°C/Gas 5 and roast for a further $1\frac{1}{2}$ hours. Using a metal spatula, carefully lift the pork belly and turn skin side up, without damaging the skin. Return to the oven for a further 15 minutes or until nicely crispy. Set aside to rest in a warm place for 15 minutes while you make the sauce.

Heat 1 tbsp of the olive oil in a heavy-based frying pan and fry the shallots over a high heat for 5 minutes, stirring constantly. Add the sherry vinegar; it will immediately evaporate. Add the red wine and thyme leaves and let bubble until reduced by half. Finally, whisk in the rest of the olive oil. Season with salt and pepper to taste.

Cut the pork belly into portions and serve with the sauce and Olive oil mash (see page 136).

Serves 6–8
$\frac{1}{2}$ belly of pork (free-range organic pork, preferably rare breed), about 2kg
light olive oil for oiling
sea salt and freshly ground pepper
2 tsp cumin seeds
bunch of thyme, leaves stripped

for the sauce
100ml olive oil
2 shallots, peeled and sliced into 5mm rings
2 tsp sherry vinegar
250ml red wine
4 thyme sprigs, leaves stripped

pinchos MORUNOS

We have modified this classic pork recipe, keeping the fillets in pieces, rather than cutting them into cubes, so the 'pinchos' or skewers from which the dish takes its name are redundant. We always use Iberico pork, which can safely be cooked pink. Olive oil mash (see page 136) and Roasted pepper salad (see page 140) are excellent accompaniments.

Trim the pork of any fat or sinews, then cut each fillet into 4 equal lengths, on the diagonal. Place in a large bowl or plastic tub and pour over the olive oil, then sprinkle with the spices, dried oregano, garlic and salt and pepper. Toss well, then cover and leave to marinate in the fridge for 24 hours.

Preheat your griddle until smoking (or light your barbecue and wait until the coals burn white). Remove the pork from the marinade, strain the liquor and reserve. Cook the pork on the griddle (or barbecue) for 8–10 minutes, turning every couple of minutes and basting with the marinade from time to time.

Transfer the pork to a warm platter and leave to rest in a warm place (or warming oven at 50°C) for 20 minutes before serving. Garnish with fresh oregano sprigs if available.

Serves 4

1.5kg Iberico pork fillets (tenderloins)
150ml light olive oil
2 tsp smoked paprika
1 tsp ground cumin
1 tsp dried oregano
1 head of garlic, separated into cloves, peeled and smashed
sea salt and freshly ground pepper
oregano sprigs, to garnish (optional)

BRAISED + pig cheeks

We have only discovered this cut of pork relatively recently, but it has become one of our favourites. The meat is quite dark and could be mistaken for shin of beef, which incidentally would be a fine substitute if you can't get pig cheeks. We like to serve this robust dish with Olive oil mash (see page 136) and a bottle of full-bodied red wine.

Serves 6–8

2kg pig cheeks (or shin of beef, cut
  into large pieces)
light olive oil for cooking
1 onion, peeled and sliced
1 carrot, peeled and sliced
2 celery sticks, sliced
1 leek, trimmed and sliced
3 garlic cloves, peeled and chopped
2 tbsp tomato purée
finely pared zest of ½ orange
  (in one piece)
3 tbsp sherry vinegar
1 bottle of red wine
1 star anise
3 cloves
1 thyme sprig
1 bay leaf
sea salt and freshly ground pepper

Preheat the oven to 150°C/Gas 2. Trim the pig cheeks of any fat or sinew and carefully pat dry with kitchen paper. Heat a little olive oil in a large, flameproof casserole and brown the pig cheeks in batches on all sides. Remove with a slotted spoon and set aside.

Add a little more oil to the casserole if necessary and gently fry the onion, carrot, celery, leek and garlic over a medium-low heat for about 20 minutes or until softened and well browned. Add the tomato purée and orange zest, and continue to fry for 5 minutes. Add the sherry vinegar, scraping the bottom of the casserole to deglaze as it evaporates.

Then add the red wine, star anise, cloves, thyme and bay leaf. Bring to the boil, skimming off any scum that rises to the surface, then return the pig cheeks to the casserole. Cover the casserole with a piece of baking paper cut to fit and with a 2cm hole cut out from the centre (to let steam escape). Place the casserole in the oven and cook for 2½ hours. Lift out the pig cheeks on to a warm platter, cover and keep warm.

For a refined version, pass the cooking liquor through a sieve into a saucepan, pressing the vegetables in the sieve with the back of a wooden spoon. Bring the liquor to the boil and let bubble until reduced by half and then season with salt and pepper to taste. For a more rustic version, simply strain the liquor, reserving the vegetables and return to the sauce after reducing it.

Cut the pig cheeks into 1cm thick slices and serve with lots of sauce.

note This recipe also works extremely well if you cook the casserole overnight in a very low temperature oven. Heat the oven to 75°C (rather than 150°C) and cook for 12 hours.

+albondigas

This classic dish of meatballs with tomato sauce can be, and often is, very disappointing. However, this superior recipe from our head chef, Jean Philippe Patruno, is excellent. We suggest you buy a piece of fillet and hand chop it yourself just before cooking, so you can achieve the right texture and be sure it is very fresh. This way, you can serve the albondigas pink in the middle, as we do. If you don't want to mince the beef yourself, choose a nice piece of fillet from your butcher and ask him to do it for you. He should also be able to supply the caul fat. The accompanying tomato sauce is quite spicy; if you don't like the heat, reduce or leave out the cayenne and chillies.

Serves 6

for the albondigas
1 bundle of caul fat
800g fillet of beef
1 tsp ground cumin
2 tsp cayenne pepper
10g sea salt
4 turns fresh black pepper
30g fresh breadcrumbs
1 free-range egg, beaten
2–3 tbsp light olive oil

for the tomato sauce
3 tbsp light olive oil
1 Spanish onion, peeled and chopped
4 garlic cloves, peeled and thinly sliced
1 large thyme sprig
2 bay leaves
2 large red chillies, deseeded and diced
1 green pepper, cored, deseeded and diced
1 red pepper, cored, deseeded and diced
1 tsp sweet paprika
1 tsp cayenne pepper
400g can peeled plum tomatoes
1 tbsp tomato purée
sea salt and freshly ground pepper

Soak the caul fat in plenty of cold water for at least 1 hour. In the meantime, make the tomato sauce. Heat the olive oil in a large frying pan. Add the onion and fry over a medium heat for 5 minutes. Add the garlic, thyme and bay leaves and fry for a further 5 minutes. Add the chillies and peppers and fry for another 5 minutes, stirring occasionally.

Stir in the paprika and cayenne and cook, stirring, for 2 minutes. Add the tomatoes and bring to the boil. Lower the heat and reduce slowly for 25–30 minutes until the sauce is thick and pulpy. Season with salt and pepper to taste. Keep hot or reheat just before serving.

To make the albondigas, remove the caul fat from the water and squeeze to remove excess liquid. Using a large, sharp, heavy knife, finely chop the beef fillet; it should resemble coarsely minced beef. Place in a bowl and add the cumin, cayenne, salt, pepper and breadcrumbs. Mix thoroughly with your hands, then add the beaten egg to bind the mixture.

Stretch out a piece of the caul on a board and cut into a rectangular shape, about 12 x 7cm. Lightly roll 40g of the mince in the palm of your hand into a ball. Place the meatball on the caul fat and roll the fat around $1\frac{1}{2}$ times to enclose. Twist both loose ends of the fat to seal and cut off the excess. Shape gently in your hand and set aside. Repeat the process to use all of the meat mixture; you should have about 20 meatballs.

To cook the albondigas, heat the olive oil in a large frying pan. Add the meatballs and fry over a high heat for $2\frac{1}{2}$ minutes, turning to brown well all over. Take off the heat and leave to rest for $1\frac{1}{2}$ minutes, then serve the albondigas immediately, with the hot tomato sauce.

Meat cooked on the bone always has a better flavour than if it is cooked boneless and we are particularly partial to rib of beef. Try to find a piece of rib that has been aged properly, ideally for 3–4 weeks, and has a nice, even marbling of fat. We always look for a cut with a good dark colour and a slightly dry appearance.

The cooking time will depend on the thickness of the meat – you will need to allow a bit longer for a thicker rib. Make sure the meat is at room temperature when you cook it and allow half an hour for resting afterwards.

RIB OF beef A LAS brasas

Oil a griddle pan and heat over a high heat until it is smoking hot. Meanwhile, pat the beef dry with kitchen paper and season well with salt and pepper. Place the beef on the griddle, lower the heat slightly to medium-high and cook for 7–8 minutes on each side.

Transfer the rib to a warm serving platter, cover with foil and leave to rest in a warm place for 30 minutes.

Meanwhile, make the sauce. Gently warm the butter with the garlic and thyme in a small saucepan. Add the juices from the meat, then set aside to infuse; keep warm.

Carve the meat from the rib, arrange on warm plates and drizzle with the garlicky thyme butter. Serve with a simple salad and Fino chips with brava sauce (see page 131).

Serves 2–3

light olive oil for oiling
1 rib of beef on the bone, about 1kg and 5cm thick
sea salt and freshly ground pepper
50g butter
1 garlic clove, peeled and finely chopped
1 tsp thyme leaves

FRIT mallorquin

This classic Mallorquin dish with its robust flavours is a longstanding favourite. It makes a comforting supper on a winter's night or, for those with a strong stomach, a sustaining breakfast dish on a chilly morning. The offal of young lamb (ideally milk fed) is preferable, although extremely fresh offal from an older lamb will do. Be careful not to overcook it.

Serves 4

1 aubergine, trimmed
1 fennel bulb, trimmed
1 red pepper, cored and deseeded
1 green pepper, cored and deseeded
1 medium potato, peeled
100ml light olive oil
1 Spanish onion, peeled and chopped
3 garlic cloves, peeled and finely
  chopped
1 red chilli, finely chopped
1 thyme sprig
400g lamb's offal (heart, lung, liver
  and kidney), cleaned
sea salt and freshly ground pepper

Cut the aubergine and fennel into 1cm cubes and cut the peppers into 1cm squares; set aside.

Cut the potato into 1cm cubes. Heat 5 tbsp olive oil in a large, deep heavy-based frying pan. Add the potato and onion and fry over a medium heat for 10–15 minutes until they take on a little colour.

Add the aubergine, fennel, peppers, garlic, chilli and thyme and stir well. Fry over a medium heat for 30–35 minutes, stirring every few minutes, until the vegetables are nicely caramelised. Remove and drain on kitchen paper.

Meanwhile, cut the offal into 1cm pieces, keeping the liver and kidney separate. Heat the remaining olive oil in another heavy-based frying pan over a high heat until it is almost smoking. Add the heart and lungs and fry, stirring, for 1 minute. Add the liver and kidney and sauté for a further 1 minute.

Add the vegetables to the offal and mix well, seasoning with salt and pepper to taste. Serve immediately.

MILK-FED lamb CUTLETS

Milk-fed lamb is very different to more mature, grass-fed lamb and therefore requires different treatment. The cutlets are a great delicacy and wonderful as a tapa, or as a main course. No knives or forks needed...fingers only!

Trim the cutlets neatly, removing any excess fat. Heat the olive oil in a large frying pan over a high heat. Add the cutlets, making sure they are all lying flat in the pan. Add the garlic and cook for 1 minute, then turn the cutlets over and fry for 1 minute on the other side until nicely coloured.

Remove from the heat, season with salt and pepper and scatter the chopped parsley and thyme over the cutlets. Serve immediately.

Serves 4 (or 8 as a tapa)

16–20 milk-fed lamb cutlets
20ml good quality olive oil
3 garlic cloves, peeled and chopped
sea salt and freshly ground pepper
1 tbsp finely chopped flat leaf parsley
few small thyme sprigs

kidneys ON TOAST

This is a wonderfully soothing dish for a winter supper, with a glass or two of good red wine. Really fresh, perfectly cooked kidneys are a gastronomic delight. Only buy kidneys that look red and fresh (reject any that are greyish brown) and avoid over-cooking them at all costs.

Heat 2 tbsp olive oil in a large, heavy-based frying pan, add the onions and fry gently over a low heat for about 45 minutes until deep brown and caramelised, seasoning with a little salt and pepper.

Meanwhile, remove the outer membrane from the kidneys, halve them horizontally and snip out the white sinews with kitchen scissors. Carefully pat the kidneys dry with kitchen paper.

Heat the remaining 2 tbsp olive oil in a large, heavy-based frying pan until just beginning to smoke. Add the kidneys and fry quickly over a high heat for 2 minutes on each side, seasoning as you go. Transfer them to a warm plate, cover and leave to rest in a warm place for 5 minutes.

Pour the wine into the pan, scraping up the sediment, then return to a high heat and reduce by half. Meanwhile, toast the bread on both sides. Add the juices from the rested kidneys to the liquor and check the seasoning, then pour on to the caramelised onions and stir well.

Lay two slices of toast on each plate, pile the onions on top, then add the kidneys and sprinkle with a little chopped parsley. Serve at once.

Serves 4

4 tbsp light olive oil
4 large onions, peeled and thinly sliced
sea salt and freshly ground pepper
12 lamb's kidneys
125ml red wine
8 slices of good bread
finely chopped flat leaf parsley, to serve

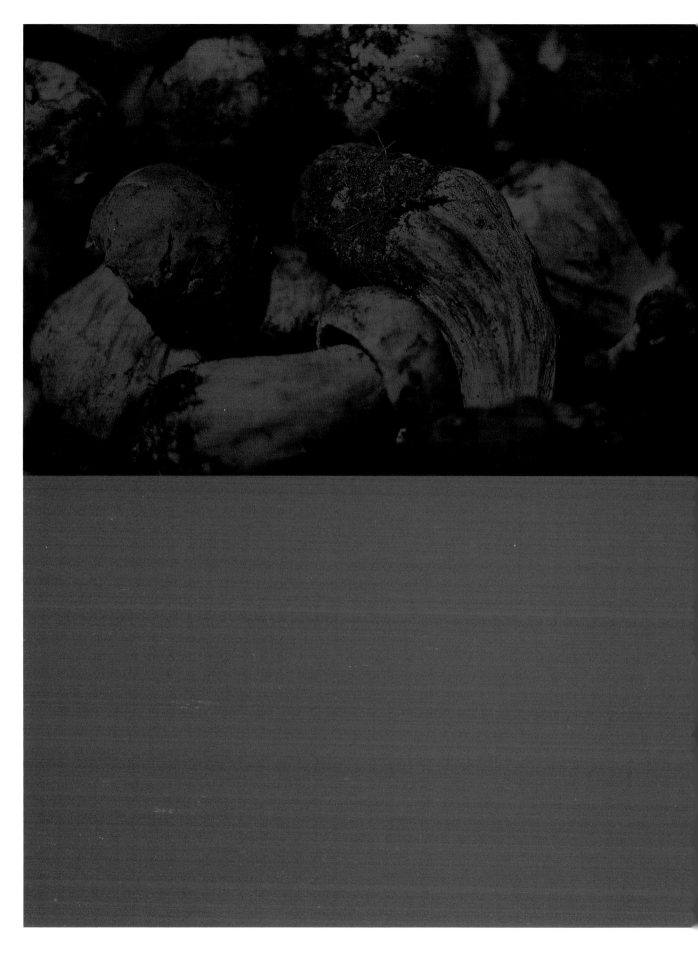

Vegetables & Salads

STUFFED
courgette
✚ flowers

We cherish the arrival of the short courgette flower season. Stuffed with goat's cheese and fried in an extra light batter, these delicate flowers make a perfect starter or simple tapa. You could even serve 3 or 4 per person with a salad for lunch. Use a Spanish goat's cheese if possible, Mont Enebro is a good choice.

Check that the courgette flowers are clean. Mix the goat's cheese with the thyme and pepper to taste. Carefully stuff the flowers with this mixture, wrapping the petals around the stuffing to keep it in place.

Sift the flour into a mixing bowl and gradually whisk in the water to make a light batter. Heat the oil in a suitable pan to 180°C. A few at a time, dip the stuffed flowers into the batter to coat and then immerse in the hot oil. Deep-fry for 3 minutes until crisp and golden. Remove with a slotted spoon, drain on kitchen paper and serve at once.

Serves 5 as a starter (10 as a tapa)

10 courgette flowers
300g goat's cheese (preferably Spanish)
2 tsp thyme leaves
freshly ground pepper
170g plain flour
500ml water
vegetable oil for deep-frying

We love asparagus but wait patiently until the home-grown vegetable is available in April before putting it on the menu. Imports from foreign climes are no match, so enjoy its magic, albeit for a short time. This recipe is very simple but the flavour combination of slightly charred asparagus, roasted almonds and lemon juice is wonderful.

PAN-FRIED ✚
asparagus
AND
almonds

Serves 4 as a starter

100g blanched almonds
28 asparagus spears
3 tbsp light olive oil
½ lemon
sea salt and freshly ground pepper

Preheat the oven to 180°C/Gas 4. Spread out the nuts on a baking tray and toast them in the oven for about 10 minutes, turning once or twice until golden brown. Tip on to a clean, dry tea-towel, wrap and allow to cool. Smash the cooled almonds with a rolling pin until broken into small pieces and keep to one side.

Trim the asparagus and peel the lower end of the stalks with a vegetable peeler. Place a large frying pan over a high heat. Add the olive oil and heat until almost smoking. Add the asparagus spears and fry for 2–3 minutes on each side until tender and just starting to char at the edges. Squeeze over the lemon juice, add the almonds and season with salt and pepper. Turn the asparagus in the juices and serve immediately.

ceps + WITH fried QUAIL'S eggs

This wonderful starter also makes an excellent brunch. When buying the ceps, check carefully that they are not wet. If they have been picked on a rainy day, the ceps may be mushy because they've soaked up a lot of water and twice as heavy – a big disadvantage considering they cost up to £40 per kilo. It is not unheard of for unscrupulous mushroom dealers to wet prized mushrooms purposely to increase their weight...

Serves 4 as a starter

400g fresh ceps
3–4 tbsp olive oil
2 garlic cloves, peeled and finely chopped
sea salt and freshly ground pepper
12 quail's eggs
a little chopped flat leaf parsley

to serve

4 slices of good quality sourdough or pain de campagne bread, toasted
extra virgin olive oil, to drizzle

To clean the ceps, firstly peel off the muddy bits of the stem as thinly as possible. Then gently scrub the ceps with a damp mushroom brush or small toothbrush to remove all grit. Gently dry with kitchen paper. Cut the ceps into 7–8mm thick slices.

In a large, heavy-based frying pan (or better still, a plancha), heat about 2 tbsp olive oil until hot. You may need to cook the ceps in batches, depending on the size of the pan or plancha. Carefully fry them for about 2 minutes on each side until golden brown, adding the garlic and seasoning halfway through cooking.

Heat another heavy-based frying pan, add 1–2 tbsp olive oil and then carefully fry the quail's eggs until cooked, about 2 minutes. Season with salt and pepper to taste.

Arrange the fried ceps on warm plates with the fried quail's eggs alongside. Spoon the fried garlic and pan juices next to the ceps and sprinkle with a little parsley. Serve immediately, accompanied by the warm toast drizzled with extra virgin olive oil.

picos + CHEESE AND chicory SALAD

Picos de Europa cheese is an excellent blue cheese from the mountain range of the same name in northern Spain. If you cannot find it, substitute Roquefort or a piece of good Stilton.

Trim the bases of the chicory bulbs, separate the leaves and place in a big bowl. Crumble the blue cheese and add to the chicory with the chopped walnuts. With your hands, roughly tear the parsley leaves into smaller bits and add to the bowl.

Drizzle with the olive oil, sherry vinegar and lemon juice, and season with salt and pepper. Toss lightly to serve.

Serves 4 as a starter

4 heads of chicory
200g blue cheese (preferably Picos)
100g walnuts, roughly chopped
small handful of flat leaf parsley
4 tbsp extra virgin olive oil
4 tsp sherry vinegar
squeeze of lemon juice
sea salt and freshly ground pepper

BABY artichokes WITH MANCHEGO +

This is a lovely way to serve tender baby artichokes on sale early in the season. The sharpness of the vinegar combined with the nuttiness of the artichoke and the saltiness of the cheese is superb. This dish also works well as part of a cold summer spread.

Serves 4 as a starter

16 baby artichokes
about 750ml vegetable oil
3 tbsp light olive oil

for the dressing
40ml sherry vinegar
50ml extra virgin olive oil
sea salt and freshly ground pepper

to serve
Manchego cheese

First make the dressing. Bring the sherry vinegar to the boil in a saucepan and reduce by half, then pour into a small bowl. Add the extra virgin olive oil and whisk to combine. Season with salt and pepper; set aside.

To prepare the artichokes, remove all the coarse outer leaves. Using a sharp knife, peel the stalks and cut off the top 2–3cm of the leaves. Heat the vegetable oil in a large saucepan (big enough to hold all the artichokes) to 80–90°C (no hotter). Immerse the artichokes in the oil and cook for 25–30 minutes, maintaining the same temperature (use a thermometer). Remove the artichokes with a slotted spoon and place, heads down, on a wire rack over the sink for 10 minutes to drain off most of the oil.

Cut the artichokes in half lengthways. Heat the light olive oil in a large pan and fry the artichoke halves, flat side down for 2–3 minutes until starting to brown. Whisk the dressing to re-combine. Place the artichokes on a warm serving plate and drizzle with the dressing. Using a vegetable peeler, shave Manchego over the artichokes, then eat straight away.

ENSALADILLA
russa +

Russian salad is a retro Spanish classic; its popularity was at a peak during the war years as it could be put together using ingredients entirely out of a can. It can be (and often is) repulsive. However, if you use fresh vegetables and a home-made mayonnaise it is truly delicious. For a mayonnaise with a fine, delicate flavour, it is important to use a light olive oil rather than a strong, green oil.

First make the mayonnaise. Put the egg yolks into a large mixing bowl with a pinch of salt, two turns of black pepper and the mustard and whisk together. Start to add the olive oil very slowly, drizzle by drizzle, whisking continuously, until the mixture begins to thicken. Continue adding the olive oil, now in a thin stream, whisking all the time. Finally, whisk in the lemon juice and wine vinegar. Cover the bowl with cling film and refrigerate until needed.

To prepare the salad, cook the carrots, peas, green beans and new potatoes separately in boiling salted water, keeping them slightly crunchy. Refresh under cold water, drain and keep to one side. Slice the spring onions and gherkins into rounds. Cut the piquillo peppers into strips. Roughly chop the hard-boiled eggs.

Combine the par-boiled vegetables, spring onions, gherkins, piquillo peppers, eggs, capers and parsley in a large bowl and toss to mix. Add the mayonnaise and toss well to coat all the vegetables. Season the salad with salt and plenty of black pepper. Refrigerate until needed. Serve with crusty bread.

Serves 4 as a side dish or tapa

2 large carrots, peeled and diced

100g peas (preferably fresh, otherwise frozen)

100g green beans, topped, tailed and cut in half

500g baby new potatoes, peeled and diced

1 small bunch of spring onions, trimmed

7 gherkins

2 red piquillo peppers

4 hard-boiled eggs, shelled

2 tbsp capers, drained

2 tbsp finely chopped flat leaf parsley

sea salt and freshly ground pepper

for the mayonnaise

3 egg yolks

sea salt and freshly ground pepper

1½ tsp Dijon mustard

350ml light olive oil

juice of ½ lemon

4 tsp white wine vinegar

Calcots are a large variety of spring onion, about the size of a small leek. In Catalunya, large calcot parties or 'calcotadas' are held when the vegetable is in season. At these, the onions are grilled over hot coals and eaten in prodigious quantities. Calcots are difficult to come by, but a large spring onion is a suitable alternative (a small leek is not). There are many different ways to make the sauce, but this is our favourite.

calcots+ WITH salbitxada

Serves 4

4 bunches of calcots or fat
  spring onions

for the sauce
20 hazelnuts
20 blanched almonds
about 300ml olive oil
2 garlic bulbs, divided into cloves and
  peeled
2 tomatoes, quartered, deseeded and
  roughly chopped
handful of flat leaf parsley
pinch of cayenne pepper
3 tsp sherry vinegar
6 tbsp olive oil
sea salt and freshly ground pepper

First, preheat the oven to 180°C/Gas 4. Spread out the hazelnuts and almonds on a baking tray and toast in the oven for about 10 minutes, turning them once or twice until nicely browned, taking care not to let any burn. Allow to cool.

Heat the barbecue or preheat a griddle pan until smoking, then char-grill the onions, in batches if necessary, for 10 minutes or so, turning every so often. Remove from the heat and place in a deep dish, then cover with cling film and leave to steam while you make the sauce.

Meanwhile, in a small saucepan, heat about 200ml olive oil (enough to completely cover the garlic when it is added) to 80°C, no hotter. Add the garlic cloves and cook (or confit) at this temperature for 15 minutes (use a thermometer to check). Remove with a slotted spoon and drain.

Rub the hazelnuts in a cloth to remove the skins, then place in a blender with the almonds and whiz until coarsely ground. Add the garlic, tomatoes and parsley and blitz again. Transfer the mixture to a bowl and stir in the cayenne, sherry vinegar and olive oil. Season the sauce with salt and pepper to taste.

Serve the calcots while still warm, accompanied by the sauce.

FINO
+ chips
WITH
brava SAUCE

Our recipe departs from traditional 'patatas bravas' because we fry the potatoes in the shape of chips rather than wedges or cubes, and we serve the sauce on the side rather than poured over the potatoes, which makes them soggy. Much has been written on the variety of potato that makes the best chips. Maris Piper and Desirée are often mentioned as good possibilities, but in reality different potatoes respond favourably to frying at different times of the year. We suggest that you get to know a good greengrocer, who should be able to tell you which variety to choose at any particular time.

To make the brava sauce, heat the olive oil in a medium saucepan and fry the onion over a low heat for 5 minutes until softened. Add the garlic and fry for another 5 minutes. Add the diced peppers and fry, stirring occasionally, for 10 minutes. Add the cayenne, paprika, chilli and tomato purée and fry, stirring, for 5 minutes.

Add the sugar, bay leaf, thyme and canned tomatoes. Bring to a gentle simmer and cook over a low heat for 40 minutes. Discard the herbs, season with salt and pepper to taste and set aside.

For the chips, peel the potatoes and cut them into chips, 1.5cm thick and all roughly the same size. Put into a bowl and rinse under cold running water for 5 minutes or so, to get rid of any excess starch. Drain well and pat dry in a clean tea-towel.

Heat the oil in a deep-fryer to 150°C. Fry the chips in batches for 7 minutes, then remove, drain and pat dry with kitchen paper. Leave the chips to cool completely (even better, refrigerate them for 30 minutes).

Heat the oil again, this time to 180°C. Fry the chips in batches for 5–7 minutes until golden and crisp, then drain and pat dry on kitchen paper. Put into a warm bowl and toss with the garlic, thyme leaves and sea salt. Serve the chips with the hot Brava sauce on the side.

Serves 4

for the brava sauce
2 tbsp light olive oil
1 onion, peeled and diced
2 garlic cloves, peeled and sliced
1 red pepper, cored, deseeded and diced
1 green pepper, cored, deseeded and diced
1 tsp cayenne pepper
pinch of spicy paprika
1 red chilli, deseeded and diced
2 tsp tomato purée
pinch of sugar
1 bay leaf
1 thyme sprig
400g can peeled plum tomatoes
sea salt and freshly ground pepper

for the fino chips
1.5kg potatoes (suitable for chips)
vegetable oil for deep-frying
1 garlic clove, peeled and crushed
1 thyme sprig, leaves stripped
sea salt

olives AND OLIVE OIL

Spain is the largest producer of olive oil in Europe and olive trees have been cultivated ever since the Phoenicians introduced them around 1100 BC. Olives are produced for the table as well as for their oil and there are many different varieties. Unripe olives are green, firm-fleshed and tend to be bitter. As the olives ripen they turn from green to purple and become oilier. Ripe olives are black, with little or no bitterness.

Choose olives that are cured in brine in preference to those immersed solely in olive oil as the oil causes them to deteriorate. Store bottled olives in the fridge once they are opened; similarly those bought in tubs from a delicatessen. Large, sweet green Manzanilla, tasty green Gordal, black Hojiblanca and tiny slightly bitter Arbequina, are some of our favourite varieties. Served with cold meats and accompanied by a glass of crisp, cold Manzanilla sherry, fine olives are a real treat, and, of course, they are indispensable in cooking.

Locating really good olive oil can be, and often is, a minefield. If possible, find a reliable delicatessen or market where you can taste the oils and choose those you like. Positive qualities to look for are fruitiness, pungency and bitterness. Avoid oils that are in any way musty or winey. Also read the labels carefully. Estate bottled oils are likely to be superior to those bottled commercially. Check to see whether the oil was produced and bottled by the same setup – a good sign. Olive oil is best consumed young after bottling, so don't buy an oil that is older than 18 months. At home, store olive oils in a cool, dark place and try to consume within a few months of opening.

There are three main olive oil qualities and we recommend that you keep all three in your kitchen cupboard as they have different applications.

Aceite de oliva virgen extra is the highest quality of Spanish olive oil. It is guaranteed to be cold pressed and must not exceed an acidity level of 1g fatty acid per 100ml of oil. This oil should be used only when the taste will be entirely appreciated – on salads and vegetables, with bread, over cold meats, freshly marinated anchovies, gazpacho and cheese, drizzled over finished dishes (hot or cold)...and so on. Don't use it for frying or in dishes where the flavour will be overpowered by other ingredients. We avoid using this olive oil even in salad dressings that contain mustard, because its flavour would be lost.

Aceite de oliva virgen is the second best quality of Spanish olive oil, guaranteed to be cold pressed and with a maximum acidity level of 2g fatty acid per 100ml of oil. We use this olive oil for the same purposes as *aceite de oliva virgen extra* if we are not looking to lend a particularly special flavour to the dish. We also use it for frying where the dish really benefits from a more superior oil than a straightforward *aceite de oliva* – to cook tortillas, Patatas a lo pobre (see page 134), paella, roasted red peppers and fish 'a la plancha', for example.

Aceite de oliva is refined olive oil or a blend of refined and cold pressed oils, but has less flavour than cold pressed oils. This oil is perfect for cooking if you wish to add minimal flavour to a dish. It is also ideal for a mildly flavoured mayonnaise and tartare sauce, and is suitable for deep-frying.

For some purposes, **we mix different olive oils** or combine one with another type of oil to achieve a different flavour. For example, a strong green olive oil can be too pungent for a mayonnaise, while a mixture of *aceite de oliva virgen extra* and *aceite de oliva virgen* is generally better. Equally in a salad dressing, you may prefer a mixture of *aceite de oliva virgen* and a nut oil. **Get to know your oils** and experiment with the way you use them.

patatas
A LO POBRE +

Literally 'poor man's potatoes', this dish is truly delicious. It is a wonderful combination of caramelised vegetable flavours and makes an excellent accompaniment to a whole host of meat and fish dishes. Don't be tempted to cut corners and rush the cooking procedure, the magic comes with the slow caramelisation of the vegetables.

Preheat the oven to 180°C/Gas 4. Heat the olive oil in a large, ovenproof frying pan over a medium heat. Add the chopped onions and fry for 10–15 minutes, turning occasionally.

In the meantime, cut the peppers into 1cm strips. Peel the potatoes and cut into 1cm thick slices. Add the garlic to the onions and fry for 2 minutes. Add the pepper strips with the bay leaves and thyme sprigs and fry for 6 minutes, stirring occasionally. Add the potato slices, mix well and fry for a further 5 minutes.

Transfer the frying pan to the oven and cook for 10 minutes. Remove the pan from the oven, stir the vegetables well, then return to the oven and bake for a further 10 minutes. Season with salt and pepper to taste and scatter the parsley and thyme over the caramelised vegetables. Serve straight away.

Serves 4 as a side dish

200ml light olive oil
3 onions, peeled and chopped
2 large red peppers, cored and deseeded
2 large green peppers, cored and deseeded
1kg Desirée or waxy potatoes
3 garlic cloves, peeled and sliced lengthways
2 bay leaves
1 large thyme sprig, plus extra leaves to garnish
sea salt and freshly ground pepper
2 tbsp chopped flat leaf parsley

olive OIL
mash

This mash is wonderfully comforting, especially on a cold winter's night, and it is an ideal accompaniment to crisp pork belly, pinchos morunos, lamb or indeed almost any dish we can think of. If you cannot find King Edward potatoes, choose another variety recommended for mashing. Some people seem to enjoy the drudgery of a hand-held potato masher, but in our opinion, a potato ricer or a mouli-legumes makes for a better result and a more enjoyable experience.

Serves 4 as a side dish

1kg King Edward potatoes, peeled
sea salt and freshly ground pepper
250ml single cream
2 garlic cloves, peeled and crushed
160g unsalted butter, diced
50ml extra virgin olive oil

Cut the potatoes into even-sized pieces and boil in salted water until tender; drain. Slowly heat the cream in another pan, removing it from the heat just before it comes to the boil.

Crush the boiled potatoes through a potato ricer or a mouli-legumes into a warm, large mixing bowl and add the garlic and hot cream, stirring constantly with a wooden spoon.

Add the butter and continue stirring, then add the olive oil and season with salt and pepper to taste. Serve immediately.

spinach, PINE NUTS AND raisins ✚

This works equally well as a vegetable side dish or vegetarian tapa. Fresh baby spinach leaves hardly need to be cooked at all, just softened slightly in a hot pan. Avoid overcooking at all costs.

Put the raisins into a small dish, add 2 tsp sherry vinegar and set aside to soak for 10 minutes.

Heat a large, heavy based frying pan over a medium heat. Add the olive oil and heat until smoking. Add the pine nuts, shallot and raisins and fry for 2 minutes. Throw in the spinach leaves, immediately remove from the heat and stir for 15 seconds – just so the spinach wilts a tiny bit.

Tip into a warm bowl to stop the spinach from overcooking. Season with salt and pepper to taste, drizzle with the remaining sherry vinegar and serve at once.

Serves 4 as a side dish

20g raisins
5 tsp sherry vinegar
2 tbsp light olive oil
30g pine nuts
1 small shallot, peeled and finely diced
500g baby spinach leaves, washed and well drained
sea salt and freshly ground pepper

green ✚ BEANS AND shallots

We were initially surprised when guests at Fino waxed lyrical about such a simple dish. Perhaps because green beans are usually served with just a little butter and seasoning, our beans stand out from the crowd.

Cook the green beans in lightly salted boiling water for 2–3 minutes; they should still be a little crunchy. Drain and refresh in cold water. Drain thoroughly and set aside.

Heat the olive oil and butter in a frying pan over a medium heat. Add the garlic and shallots and fry for $\frac{1}{2}$ minute. Add the beans and sauté for $1\frac{1}{2}$ minutes. Add the chopped parsley, season with salt and pepper and serve immediately.

Serves 4 as a side dish

250g green beans, topped and tailed
sea salt and freshly ground pepper
1 tbsp light olive oil
25g unsalted butter
1 garlic clove, peeled and finely chopped
1½ shallots, peeled and finely chopped
2 tsp finely chopped flat leaf parsley

BROAD beans AND jamón

We always look forward to the broad bean season. The first to arrive at the restaurant are from North Africa in March. Our source gradually works northwards until June and July when we get English broad beans – the best of all. Skinning broad beans is a rather laborious task. We recommend you grab an assistant or two and a glass of something, put on some good music and peel away.

Heat the olive oil in a large frying pan over a medium heat. Add the shallot and jamón and sauté for 2–3 minutes.

Add the water and simmer to reduce a little, then add the broad beans and cook for 3 minutes, turning them occasionally.

Add the shredded mint and season with salt and pepper to taste. Toss well to mix and serve, sprinkled with a few mint leaves.

Serves 4 as a starter or side dish

1–2 tbsp olive oil
1 shallot, peeled and finely diced
80g jamón Serrano, cut into 5mm cubes
4 tbsp water
250g podded broad beans, skinned
few mint leaves, finely shredded, plus extra to garnish
sea salt and freshly ground pepper

---

trempó

This is our favourite Mallorquin salad and we take it on family picnics in our small boat, the trempó strangely benefiting from sitting in its own juices. Generally, the Spanish are not known for fresh tasting salads, more often choosing to accompany meat and fish with potatoes or fried vegetables. The superior long, thin, pale green Mediterranean peppers are included in this salad. You can sometimes find them here, although green bell peppers can be used instead.

Serves 4–6 as a side dish

1kg ripe, flavourful tomatoes
1 large Spanish onion, peeled and roughly chopped
2 green peppers (preferably long, pale ones), cored and deseeded
100ml extra virgin olive oil
juice of 1 lemon
sea salt and freshly ground pepper
sprinkling of cumin seeds (optional)

Quarter the tomatoes and place in a salad bowl with the onion. Cut the green peppers lengthways into strips, add to the salad and toss together.

Whisk the olive oil and lemon juice together in a jug to make a dressing and pour over the salad. Season with salt and pepper, adding a sprinkling of cumin seeds if you like. Toss to mix and allow to stand for $\frac{1}{2}$–1 hour before serving.

ROASTED + pepper SALAD

This basic pepper salad is an excellent side dish, but it also works brilliantly as a light course in its own right if you add any combination of the following: smoked or canned anchovy fillets, toasted pine nuts, little croûtons, capers and extra freshly chopped herbs such as basil, oregano and parsley.

Serves 4 as a side dish

4 red peppers
4 green peppers
4 garlic cloves, peeled and finely sliced
4 tsp sherry vinegar
4 tbsp extra virgin olive oil
2 tsp thyme leaves
sea salt and freshly ground pepper

Preheat a griddle pan until smoking hot (or a barbecue or the grill) and char-grill the whole peppers until well blackened all over, about 15–20 minutes. Put the char-grilled peppers into a large bowl, cover with cling film and leave to steam for at least 30 minutes.

Take out the peppers and peel off the skin. Halve and remove the core and seeds, then slice the peppers lengthways into 1cm wide strips.

Put the pepper strips into a bowl with the garlic, sherry vinegar, olive oil and thyme. Toss to mix and season with salt and pepper.

Either serve warm straight away, or refrigerate for 30 minutes and serve slightly chilled.

+ LAMB'S lettuce SALAD

This might seem too simple, but for us there is no greater salad. The dressing works so well with the lamb's lettuce that we eat this every day for lunch.

Carefully wash and dry the lamb's lettuce. For the dressing, whisk the olive oil, salt and lemon juice together in a little bowl. Pour the dressing over the salad, toss well and serve.

Serves 4 as a side salad

150g lamb's lettuce (mâche)
40ml finest extra virgin olive oil
½ tsp sea salt
3 tsp lemon juice

tumbet

We have fond memories of eating this dish in Mallorca as children. It is, in our view, the best possible accompaniment to lamb. Individually frying the vegetables before assembling the tumbet is critical to the end result, so don't be tempted to skip this stage. Traditionally this dish is cooked and served in an earthenware dish, called a 'greixonera', although any ovenproof dish can be used.

For the tumbet, cut the aubergines into 1.5cm rounds and lay these out on kitchen paper. Sprinkle liberally with sea salt and leave to dégorge (draw out the bitter juices) for about 20 minutes.

Peel the potatoes and cut into 5mm thick rounds. Heat 2 tbsp of the olive oil in a large frying pan over a medium heat and fry the potato slices in batches for about 10 minutes on each side until golden brown. Drain on kitchen paper, season lightly with salt and pepper and keep to one side. (You may need to add a little more oil as you fry each batch.)

Halve, core and deseed the peppers, then slice lengthways into 1cm strips. Heat another 2 tbsp olive oil in the pan and fry the red peppers over a medium heat for 20–25 minutes, stirring occasionally. Remove and drain on kitchen paper, season lightly and keep to one side.

Meanwhile, pat the aubergine slices dry with kitchen paper to remove the salt and bitter juices. Heat the remaining 2 tbsp olive oil in another large frying pan and fry the aubergine rounds in batches, until golden brown on both sides, adding more oil as necessary with each batch. Drain the aubergines on kitchen paper and set aside.

To make the tomato sauce, briefly immerse the tomatoes in boiling water to loosen the skins, then peel. Quarter the tomatoes and remove the seeds. Heat the olive oil in a large frying pan over a medium heat. Add the onion and shallot and sweat for 15 minutes. Add the garlic, thyme, oregano and bay leaves and sweat for a further 5 minutes. Add the tomatoes, bring to a simmer and reduce slowly for 25–30 minutes, to a thick sauce. Season with salt and pepper to taste and remove the bay leaves and herb sprigs.

To bake the tumbet, preheat the oven to 180°C/Gas 4. Oil the bottom and sides of an earthenware (or other) ovenproof dish. Layer the potato slices over the bottom of the dish. Cover with the red pepper strips, then layer the aubergine slices on top. Pour the tomato sauce over the top of the dish and bake for 25 minutes. Serve immediately.

Serves 6 as a side dish

for the tumbet
2 large aubergines, trimmed
sea salt and freshly ground pepper
1kg Maris Piper potatoes
about 6 tbsp light olive oil
2 large red peppers

for the tomato sauce
14 plum tomatoes
2 tbsp light olive oil
½ onion, peeled and chopped
1 shallot, peeled and finely chopped
2 garlic cloves, peeled and thinly sliced
1 large thyme sprig
1 oregano sprig
2 bay leaves

coca
+ MALLORQUIN

We have fond memories of eating this Spanish-style pizza while on holiday with our family in Mallorca. Surprisingly, perhaps, it dates back further than the more familiar Italian pizza. The simplicity of this recipe is its appeal, though you can add other flavourings, such as anchovies and olives if you like. It is equally delicious eaten hot or cold on a scorching summer's day. This recipe makes two cocas that will fit into a domestic oven.

**Serves 6 as a main course
(or many more as a tapa)**

for the dough
500g plain flour, plus extra for dusting
1 tsp salt
260ml lukewarm water
10g fresh yeast (or 5g dried)
pinch of caster sugar
3 tbsp olive oil, plus extra for oiling
2½ tbsp Manzanilla sherry or
  white wine

for the topping
3 green peppers
2 red peppers
4 tbsp light olive oil
3 medium onions, peeled and chopped
25 very ripe plum tomatoes or
  50 cherry tomatoes
sea salt and freshly ground pepper
4 tsp thyme leaves
35ml good quality extra virgin olive oil
1 garlic clove, peeled and finely
  chopped
4 bay leaves (optional)
2 tbsp roughly torn fresh oregano

To make the dough, sift the flour and salt into a large bowl and make a well in the middle. Put 2 tbsp of the warm water in a small bowl, crumble in the fresh yeast (or sprinkle in dried), add the sugar and stir to dissolve. Pour the yeast liquid into the flour well, cover it with some of the flour from around the edges and set aside for 15 minutes.

Add the olive oil, sherry and remaining water. Mix the ingredients together and knead to a smooth dough. Cover the bowl with cling film and leave in a warm place for about 1 hour until doubled in size.

Preheat the oven to 180°C/Gas 4. Put the peppers on a roasting tray, drizzle with 2 tbsp of the light olive oil and roast for 30 minutes, turning once or twice. Transfer the peppers to a bowl, cover with cling film and leave to steam for 15 minutes.

Meanwhile, heat 1 tbsp light olive oil in a large frying pan, add the chopped onions and fry over a medium heat for 15–20 minutes, stirring frequently. Remove and keep to one side.

Preheat the grill. Halve the tomatoes lengthways, arrange cut side up on a baking tray and drizzle with a little light olive oil. Season with salt and pepper and sprinkle with the thyme. Grill the tomatoes for 5 minutes until they begin to soften, then set aside.

Take out the peppers and peel off the skin. Halve and remove the core and seeds, then slice the peppers lengthways into 1cm wide strips.

Preheat the oven to 180°C/Gas 4. Turn out the dough on to a lightly floured surface and knead again. Then divide in half and roll out each piece to a rectangle, about 25 x 40cm. Lift each rectangle on to a lightly oiled baking tray and prick the dough with a fork, leaving a 3cm border unpricked around the edge. Mix 2 tsp of the extra virgin olive oil with the garlic and brush over the dough.

Layer the onions, pepper strips and tomatoes evenly over the dough, leaving a 3cm margin clear at the edges. Add the bay leaves if using and oregano, season with salt and pepper and drizzle with the remaining extra virgin olive oil. Bake in the oven for 25 minutes. Serve hot or cold.

Desserts

CARAMELISED
+orange
SALAD

This is a very simple, yet delicious orange salad. The zest is particularly crunchy and provides a wonderful contrast to the succulent oranges and sweet liqueur flavoured syrup. Seek out the very best oranges you can find in season.

Serves 4

5 large, top quality oranges
75g caster sugar
25ml Grand Marnier
25ml Cointreau
caster sugar for dusting

Using a sharp knife, finely peel the zest from 1 orange and cut into long, fine strips (julienne); set aside. Squeeze the juice from this orange and one other; set aside.

Peel the remaining 3 oranges, removing all the pith, and slice into rounds, 1cm thick. Place in a heatproof bowl.

Put the sugar in a heavy-based frying pan and warm gently until melted, then continue to cook to a light caramel. Carefully add the Grand Marnier, Cointreau and orange juice. Cook for 2 minutes to a smooth syrup and remove from the heat. Pour the hot syrup over the orange slices and leave to cool, then refrigerate.

Meanwhile, warm the oven to 50°C/lowest gas setting. Half-fill a saucepan with cold water, add the orange zest julienne and bring to the boil. Remove the zest with a slotted spoon and discard the water. Repeat this process twice more, then drain the orange zest and pat dry with kitchen paper.

Scatter the caster sugar on a plate, then roll the orange zest in the sugar to coat. Spread the zest strips out on a baking tray, making sure none of them are touching each other. Place in the oven to dry and crisp for $1\frac{1}{2}$ hours. Transfer to a wire rack to cool.

Serve the orange salad in shallow bowls, sprinkled with the candied orange zest.

figs POACHED IN red wine +

We have fond memories of being dangled by our ankles over a neighbouring farmer's wall in Mallorca to purloin juicy figs to smuggle home or eat on the way to the beach.

Using good quality wine can only help to improve the flavour of the dish, though it doesn't mean you have to raid the cellar of one of its finest bottles.

Put the wine, sugar, cinnamon and vanilla pod into a large saucepan over a medium heat until the sugar has dissolved, then increase the heat and bring to the boil.

Reduce the heat, add the figs and simmer for 8 minutes. Lift out the figs with a slotted spoon and set aside on a plate.

Boil the wine for about 15–20 minutes to reduce to a light syrup, then remove from the heat. Allow the syrup to cool a little, until warm.

Place the figs in shallow serving bowls and pour the syrup over them, including the cinnamon and vanilla for decoration. Finish with mint sprigs and serve with good vanilla ice cream.

Serves 4

500ml full-bodied red wine
125g caster sugar
1 large cinnamon stick, broken into
  4 lengths
1 vanilla pod, split and cut into
  4 pieces
8–16 fresh black figs (depending
  on size)
mint sprigs, to decorate

The dessert menu in a Spanish restaurant often consists of a generic photo sheet of ice creams and sorbets. When we were young, a speciality on that menu was a hollowed-out lemon filled with its own sorbet – a brilliant presentational idea, if only the sorbet had been any good... At Fino we've reinvented this dessert replacing the bad sorbet with a good one!

lemon SORBET

Serves 8

300g caster sugar
675ml water
8–10 lemons

In a heavy-based saucepan, slowly bring the sugar and 425ml water to the boil, stirring every so often to dissolve the sugar. Increase the heat and boil the syrup for 3 minutes, then leave to cool.

Meanwhile, make the lemon cases. Cut the tops off 8 lemons and keep aside. Then run a serrated grapefruit knife around the inside of the skin, working slowly until you have cut out all the fruit from the inside. Use a teaspoon to scrape out the remainder of the lemon from the shell.

Squeeze the juice from the scooped-out flesh and strain into a measuring jug. You need 250ml lemon juice; squeeze additional lemons if necessary. Add the remaining 250ml water to the jug. Pass the diluted lemon juice through a sieve into the cooled syrup, then pour into an ice-cream machine and churn until set. (Or freeze in a shallow container, beating a few times during freezing to break up the ice crystals.)

Fill the lemon cases with the sorbet, top with the lids and serve.

BLOOD orange SORBET

This is a superb sorbet to make during the short blood orange season, but if you've missed it, normal oranges work well too.

Put the sugar and water in a heavy-based saucepan and slowly bring to the boil, stirring every so often to encourage the sugar to dissolve. Increase the heat and boil the syrup for 3 minutes, then leave to cool. Meanwhile, make the orange cases, as for lemons (see above).

Squeeze the juice from the scooped-out flesh and strain into a measuring jug. Squeeze the juice from as many additional oranges as you need to make up to 500ml. Add the lemon juice. Pass the citrus juice through a sieve into the cooled syrup, then freeze (as above).

Fill the orange cases with the sorbet, place the lids on top and serve.

Serves 8

300g caster sugar
425ml water
10–12 blood oranges
juice of 2 lemons

almond
ICE CREAM

Serves 8

200g blanched almonds (or skinned hazelnuts)
600ml milk
100g sugar
200ml water

Preheat the oven to 180°C/Gas 4. Spread out the nuts on a baking tray and toast them in the oven for about 10 minutes, turning once or twice.

Put the milk, sugar, water and almonds in a saucepan and heat, stirring, to dissolve the sugar. Bring the mixture just to the boil, then take off the heat and leave to cool completely. Blitz thoroughly in a blender.

Pass the cooled mixture through a sieve, into a bowl, reserving the almond mixture left in the sieve. Add 50g of the almond mixture to the almond milk and pour into an ice-cream machine. Churn until thick and firm enough to scoop.

Personally, we find Pedro Ximenez sherry too sweet to drink, but poured over ice cream it is a different matter. All that raisiny sweetness with alcohol makes a delicious, if rather sweet, sauce.

PEDRO XIMENEZ
ice cream

Serves 8

180ml Pedro Ximenez sherry
175g raisins
500ml single cream
500ml milk
6 free-range egg yolks
130g caster sugar
50g liquid glucose

Pour the sherry into a small saucepan, add the raisins and leave to soak for 30 minutes. Then bring to the boil and allow to bubble until the liquor has reduced by half. Take off the heat and set aside.

In another small pan, bring the cream and milk to the boil, skim, then leave to cool. Beat the egg yolks, sugar and glucose together in a bowl. When the creamy milk is cool, beat it into the egg and sugar mixture.

Return to the pan and place over a very low heat. Cook very gently, stirring constantly, for about 5 minutes, until you have the consistency of a thin custard. Take care not to overheat otherwise the eggs will curdle. Pour into a bowl, add the sherry and raisin mixture and allow to cool, then churn in an ice-cream machine until thick and firm enough to scoop.

Serve with a small glass of cold Pedro Ximenez sherry on the side, which you can either pour over your ice cream or drink as you wish.

+leche FRITA

This set custard is a Spanish classic and it is usually eaten in very small squares. Find the best, freshest free-range eggs, as this will make a big difference to the end result.

Put the egg yolks and sugar into a large bowl with 2 tsp of the milk. Pour the rest of the milk into a heavy-based saucepan, add the lemon zest and juice and slowly bring to the boil, then remove from the heat.

Meanwhile, whisk the egg yolk and sugar mixture until light and creamy, then whisk in the cornflour, keeping the mixture smooth. Slowly pour on the hot milk, whisking all the time. Pour the mixture back into the pan and bring to the boil, stirring or whisking continuously. Cook, stirring, for 5 minutes. The custard should be very thick and smooth.

Pour the custard into a shallow baking tin, about 20 x 45cm, to a 1.5–2cm thickness, and allow to cool. Cover the tin with cling film and refrigerate for 1–2 hours until the mixture has set firm.

When ready to serve, cut the set custard into small squares or rounds, 6–7cm in diameter. Beat the eggs lightly in a shallow bowl. Sift the flour on to a plate. Heat the oil for deep-frying in a suitable pan to 180°C.

Dip the custard shapes into the beaten egg, then roll in the flour to dust all over, shaking off excess. Deep-fry in the hot oil for 2 minutes until crisp and golden brown on the surface, then remove and drain on kitchen paper. Dust with cinnamon and eat immediately.

Serves 4

12 free-range egg yolks
200g caster sugar
1 litre whole milk
finely grated zest and juice of 1 lemon
140g cornflour

to finish
2 free-range eggs
plain flour for dusting
vegetable oil for frying
ground cinnamon for dusting

Spaniards, on the whole, do not have the same fascination for desserts as the French, or even the English. In our experience, rather more emphasis is put on the enjoyment of savoury dishes and meals tend to be rounded off with a café solo and just a nibble of something sweet. 'Flan' often appears alongside the café solo and we think this is a delicious recipe. When you are making the caramel, do not let it darken too much otherwise it will be bitter – a dark oak colour is perfect, mahogany is too dark.

+ flan

Serves 6

for the custard
250ml whole milk
125ml double cream
125ml single cream
1 vanilla pod, split
4 free-range eggs, plus 2 egg yolks
300g caster sugar

for the caramel
250g caster sugar
3 tbsp water

Warm 6 custard cups or ramekins, measuring about 7.5cm across the top. To make the caramel, put the sugar and half of the water into a heavy-based saucepan and dissolve over a low heat, making sure the sugar melts evenly. Increase the heat to medium and boil steadily until the caramel turns a dark oak colour. Immediately take off the heat and carefully add the remaining water to stop the cooking. Stir until smooth, then pour the caramel into the moulds to a depth of about 1cm and leave to set.

Preheat the oven to 180°C/Gas 4. For the custard, pour the milk and both creams into a heavy-based saucepan, add the vanilla pod and slowly bring to the boil. Remove from the heat and set aside for 5 minutes.

In a large mixing bowl, beat the whole eggs, egg yolks and sugar together with a whisk until smooth. Strain the warm milk through a sieve into a jug or bowl, then pour on to the egg and sugar mix, whisking constantly. Leave to stand for 25 minutes, then skim the froth from the surface and allow to cool.

Pour the cooled custard mixture into the moulds, to fill them right to the top. Stand the moulds in a baking tin and surround with warm water (at about 70°C). Cook in the oven for 30–35 minutes until set. Remove the moulds from the tin and allow to cool, then refrigerate overnight or for up to 3 days.

Carefully unmould the custards just before serving. Press lightly around the edge of each custard with your thumb (to draw it away slightly from the mould) then invert on to a serving plate and tap the base of the mould until the flan falls on to the plate. Serve at once.

CREMA catalana+

We share the Spanish love for custard-based desserts and there is something particularly comforting about eating this Catalan version, with its crunchy burnt caramel topping. A chef's blow-torch is a useful tool for caramelising the topping, but if you don't have one, then use the grill preheated to its maximum setting.

Serves 4

for the custard
500ml single cream
grated zest of ½ lemon
grated zest of ½ orange
½ cinnamon stick
3 free-range egg yolks
60g caster sugar

for the caramel topping
110g caster sugar

To make the custard, pour the cream into a saucepan, add the citrus zests and cinnamon stick and heat slowly until it just comes to the boil. Remove from the heat and allow to cool for 5 minutes.

In a heatproof mixing bowl, beat the egg yolks with the caster sugar until pale and thick. Strain the warm cream through a fine sieve on to the egg yolk mixture, whisking constantly.

Set the bowl over a large saucepan of gently simmering water (or pour the custard into the top of a bain marie, set over gently simmering water in the bottom). Stir constantly with a wooden spoon until the custard thickens to the correct consistency. It should be thick enough to thinly coat the back of your spoon. You will need to be patient – this may take as long as half an hour. Remove from the heat and pour into 6 ramekins. Allow to cool and then place in the refrigerator for 1–2 hours to set.

To prepare the caramel topping, sprinkle the sugar evenly over the surface of the custards and caramelise with a blow-torch (or under a very hot grill) until the sugar turns a mahogany brown. Chill for 30 minutes before serving.

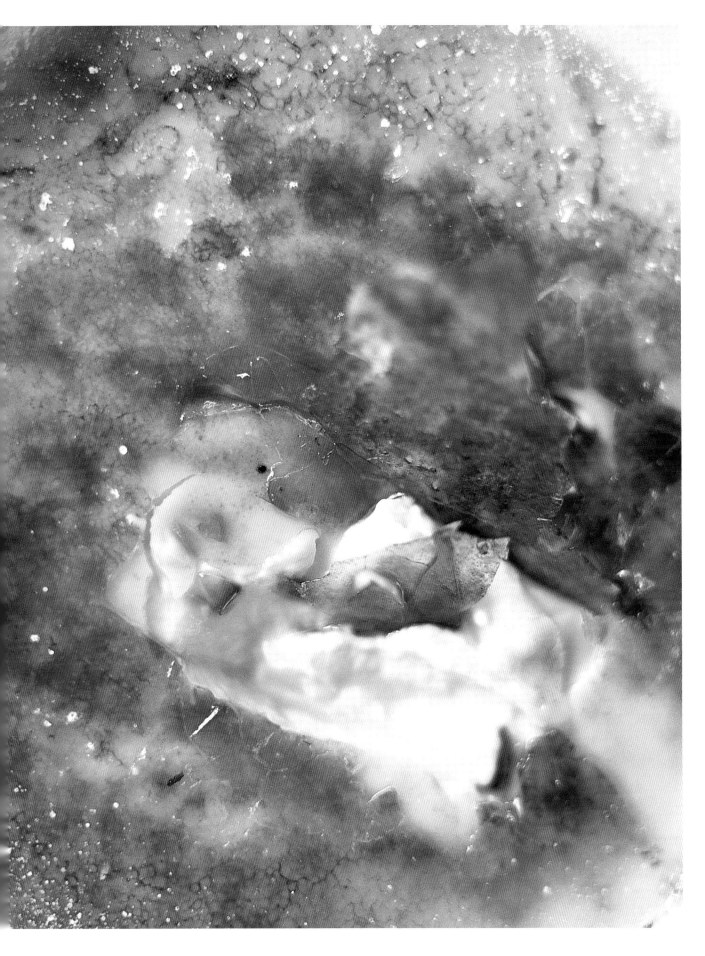

turrón SOUFFLÉ

We have always had a soft spot for turrón, an almond-based sweet from Lleida in Catalonia. It is slightly similar to nougat but with a more pronounced almond flavour and not as sweet. To make the soufflés nice and light, remember to beat the egg whites until they are really stiff. You will find this easier if the eggs are taken straight from the fridge rather than used at room temperature. And don't be tempted to open the oven door to check on the soufflés before their time is up, as this will lower the oven temperature and may impede rising. Turrón is available from all good Spanish delis.

Preheat the oven to 190°C/Gas 5. Lightly butter the insides of 4 individual 150ml soufflé dishes, using a pastry brush to work the butter upwards in vertical strokes from the bottom to the top (this will help the soufflé mixture to rise). Place the dishes in the fridge until the butter has hardened, then take them out and butter again.

Line the soufflé dishes with the chopped almonds, tilting the dishes to ensure they are evenly coated – the nuts will stick to the buttered sides as well as the bases. Return the dishes to the fridge.

Put the milk, double cream and turrón in a saucepan and slowly bring to the boil, stirring constantly so that the turrón dissolves. Take off the heat and set aside to cool for about 30 minutes.

In a separate bowl, beat the egg yolks and 80g of the caster sugar together until smooth and creamy, then beat in the cornflour, flour and salt. Gradually pour on the turrón cream, whisking all the time.

In another bowl, whisk the egg whites until they hold firm peaks. Gradually whisk in the remaining 100g sugar and continue to whisk until stiff. Gently fold the whisked egg whites into the turrón mixture until evenly incorporated.

Carefully pour the soufflé mixture into the middle of the prepared dishes and lightly smooth the top with the back of a spoon. Run your thumb around the rim of each dish, to just release the mixture from the edge. This should stop the soufflé sticking to the side of the dish and ensure that it rises evenly and straight. Stand on a baking tray and cook in the oven for 15 minutes.

Remove the soufflés from the oven, dust with icing sugar and place on dessert plates. Serve at once.

Serves 4

softened butter for greasing
30 salted almonds, roughly chopped
300ml milk
200ml double cream
180g soft turrón, roughly broken up
6 free-range eggs, separated
180g caster sugar
20g cornflour
30g plain flour
large pinch of salt
icing sugar for dusting

shots OF WHITE AND DARK chocolate

One of the most popular desserts at Fino, our shots of white and dark chocolate are the perfect 'little something sweet' when you cannot manage a full-sized dessert. The contrast of the two chocolates and the different temperatures works very well. Don't be afraid to make a good slurping sound as you suck up the last few drops...

Serves 4

for the white chocolate soup

100g best quality white chocolate
150ml single cream
100ml whole milk

for the dark chocolate

100g best quality dark chocolate
* (70% cocoa solids)*
10g cocoa powder
150ml double cream
4 tbsp whole milk

For the white chocolate soup, break up the chocolate and melt in a heatproof bowl over a saucepan of hot water on a very low heat. Take the bowl off the pan. Pour the cream and milk into a bowl. Slowly add the warm melted chocolate, stirring well until smooth, and set aside to cool. Refrigerate the white chocolate soup for 3 hours and then skim off the impurities from the surface.

For the dark chocolate layer, melt the chocolate in a heatproof bowl over a saucepan of gently simmering water. Add the cocoa powder and mix well until smooth. Pour the double cream into a large bowl and whisk until it just starts to thicken, then slowly pour in the melted chocolate, stirring well. Finally, stir in the milk to achieve a lighter consistency.

To assemble, pour the chilled white chocolate soup into 4 shot glasses, to 2–3cm from the top. Carefully spoon the dark chocolate on top of the white soup and serve, with straws.

This tart has a wonderful crumbly texture and the flavour of the almonds with just a hint of quince is fantastic. It is a favourite on our menu at Fino. In an age where we seem to be obsessed by 'food and wine matching', Santiago tart is elevated to an ecstatic level by a cold glass of semi-sweet Oloroso, the nuttiness of the sherry combining perfectly with the almonds in the tart. We think it is almost criminal to have one without the other.

SANTIAGO tart

Serves 10–12

for the sweet pastry

30g blanched almonds
225g plain flour, plus extra for dusting
100g icing sugar
pinch of salt
135g unsalted butter (at room
  temperature), plus extra for greasing
grated zest and juice of 1 lemon
1 free-range egg, beaten

for the almond filling

200g blanched almonds
grated zest and juice of 1 lemon
grated zest and juice of 1 orange
35ml amaretto liqueur
200g unsalted butter
100g icing sugar
4 free-range eggs

for the quince layer

120g quince jelly
1 tbsp water
squeeze of lemon juice

to finish

icing sugar for dusting

To make the pastry, put the almonds in a food processor and whiz until finely ground. Add the flour, icing sugar and salt and pulse briefly to mix. Add the butter and process just until the mixture resembles breadcrumbs. Add the lemon zest and juice and the egg through the feeder funnel and process briefly to a smooth, soft dough. Wrap the pastry in cling film and leave to rest in the fridge for 3 hours.

To make the almond filling, whiz the almonds in the food processor until coarsely ground. Add the citrus zests and juices with the amaretto and whiz briefly to mix. Pour into a bowl and set aside.

Put the butter and icing sugar into the food processor and whiz to mix. Add the eggs, one by one, processing briefly to combine (don't be alarmed if the mixture isn't smooth). Add this mix to the almond mixture, stir well and set aside.

Dust a cool surface with flour and roll out the pastry thinly to a large round. (You will need to keep the surface and rolling pin well floured, as this is a buttery pastry.) Lightly grease a large, loose-based tart tin, 25–30cm in diameter, and line with the pastry. Press the pastry well into the edges and trim the top edge to neaten. Leave to rest in the fridge for 20 minutes.

Preheat the oven to 180°C/Gas 4. Line the pastry case with grease-proof paper and baking beans and bake 'blind' for 15 minutes, then take out the paper and beans and bake for a further 5 minutes. Allow to cool.

For the quince layer, warm the quince jelly with the water and lemon juice in a small saucepan until melted. Pour a thin quince layer over the base of the tart and spread evenly. Spoon the almond mixture on top and smooth evenly to the edges. Bake the tart for 40–45 minutes until the filling is golden.

Leave the tart to cool in the tin for 15 minutes, then carefully remove to a large, flat plate. Dust with icing sugar and serve warm, with vanilla or almond ice cream and a glass of cold Oloroso sherry.

TARTA DE manzana

We love this very simple apple tart. Really good English Cox's apples are perfect to use, as they have a wonderful flavour and retain a good texture when baked.

Serves 4

200g ready-made puff pastry
plain flour for dusting
125g unsalted butter, softened, plus
  extra for greasing
75g caster sugar
2 tsp ground cinnamon
4 Cox's apples

Roll out the puff pastry as thinly as possible on a lightly floured surface to a large round (big enough to later cut an 18cm disc). Leave the pastry to rest for 10 minutes. Cut out the 18cm disc, using an inverted plate or flan tin base as a guide, and prick all over with a fork. Place on a lightly greased baking sheet. Preheat the oven to 180°C/Gas 4.

Melt the butter with the caster sugar and cinnamon in a small pan. Brush half of this mixture over the pastry; keep the rest to one side.

Quarter, peel and core the apples, then cut into thin slices, about 5mm thick. Arrange the apple slices in a spiral on the pastry base, radiating out from the centre and overlapping them slightly. Brush the apples with the remaining cinnamon, butter and sugar mix, then refrigerate for 30 minutes.

Bake the tart in the oven for 15 minutes or until the apples are golden and the pastry is crisp and golden brown. Serve warm, with vanilla ice cream if you like.

The origin of the ensaimada is something of a mystery. Some claim that it is derived from a Jewish cake, others that it's from an Arab dessert, but now this sweet pastry has become a Mallorquin breakfast icon. Whether the original was Jewish or Arabic, it certainly wouldn't have contained lard. Ensaimada comes in various incarnations, large or small, plain or filled with 'cabello de angel' (pumpkin jam). Our favourite is small, plain and straight from the oven. As children, and to this very day, we watch the ensaimada plate at the breakfast table like hawks – on the off chance that someone may have slept in and would not be needing theirs...

ensaimadas

Sift the flour and salt into a large bowl and stir in the caster sugar. Make a well in the middle. Crumble the fresh yeast into the warm water (or sprinkle in dried) and stir to dissolve. Pour the yeast liquid into the well, cover with a little flour from around the edge and leave for 15 minutes.

In another bowl, beat the olive oil and eggs lightly together and then add to the flour. Mix the ingredients together and work to a dough. Knead until smooth, cover the bowl with cling film and leave in a warm place for about 3 hours until doubled in size.

Turn the dough on to a lightly floured surface and knead again, then divide into 4 pieces and shape roughly into balls. Keep all but one covered with cling film. Roll out the one ball on the floured surface to a rectangle, measuring about 45 x 20cm. Lay this flat on a clean tea-towel. Spread 50g of the soft lard over the dough with your fingers and leave for 2–3 minutes.

Now start gently stretching the dough outwards with your hands, pulling the dough but maintaining a rectangular shape and taking care to avoid tearing the dough. When your rectangle is about 60 x 30cm and as thin as possible (ideally 1mm thick), gently pick up a long edge and gently roll the rectangle up into a long, thin, even sausage shape. Neatly trim the front edge. Now coil the roll into a spiral, starting tightly in the middle and keeping the seam on the underside and the edges touching as the spiral extends outwards.

Shape the other balls in the same way, cover with a clean damp cloth and leave to prove in a warm place for 4 hours.

Preheat the oven to 180°C/Gas 4. Brush the ensaimadas all over with more lard, sprinkle with a little water and dust lightly with icing sugar. Bake for 12–15 minutes until golden brown. Dust generously with icing sugar to serve.

Makes 4

500g plain flour
1 tsp salt
100g caster sugar
30g fresh yeast (or 15g dried)
150ml lukewarm water
1 tbsp olive oil
2 free-range eggs
plain flour for dusting
200g lard, softened, plus extra to glaze
icing sugar for dusting

index

suppliers

Bill's Produce Store
56 Cliffe High Street,
Lewes,
East Sussex BN7 2AN
Tel 01273 476 918
www.billsproducestore.co.uk

Real Eating Company
86–87 Western Road,
Hove,
Sussex BN3 1JB
Tel 01273 221 444
www.real-eating.co.uk

Chandos Deli
6 Princess Victoria Street,
Clifton,
Bristol BS8 4BP
Tel 01179 743 275
www.chandosdeli.com

Effings, Exeter
74 Queen Street,
Exeter, Devon EX4 3RX
Tel 01392 211 888
www.effings.co.uk

Ceci Paolo
21 High Street,
Ledbury,
Herefordshire HR8 2DS
Tel 01531 632 976
www.cecideli.co.uk

Humble Pie
Market Place, Burnham
Market, King's Lynn
Norfolk PE31 8HS
Tel 01328 738 581

THE NORTH

Appleyards
85 Wyle Cop,
Shrewsbury,
Shropshire, SY1 1UT
Tel 01743 240 180

deFine Food & Wine
Chester Road, Sandiway,
Cheshire, CW8 2NH
Tel 01606 882 101

Roberts & Speight
40 Norwood, Beverley,
East Yorkshire, HU17 9EY
Tel 01482 870 717

SCOTLAND

Heart Buchanan
380 Byres Road,
Glasgow, G12 8AR
Tel 0141 334 7626
www.heartbuchanan.co.uk

Valvona & Crolla
19 Elm Road,
Edinburgh, EH7 4AA
Tel 0131 556 6066
www.valvonacrolla.co.uk

ONLINE SHOPPING

George Scott
www.george-scott.com

Sayell Foods
www.sayellfoods.co.uk

LONDON

Brindisa
32 Exmouth Market,
Clerkenwell,
London EC1R 4QE
Tel 020 7713 1666
www.brindisa.com

Brindisa at Borough Market
The Floral Hall,
Stoney Street,
Borough Market,
London SE1
Tel 020 7407 1036
www.brindisa.com

Mortimer & Bennett
33 Turnham Green Terrace,
London W4 1RG
Tel 020 8995 4145
www.mortimerandbennett

Jeroboams W11
96 Holland Park Avenue,
London W11 3RB
Tel 020 7727 9359
www.jeroboams.co.uk

Garcia & Sons
248–250 Portobello Road,
London W11 1LL
Tel 020 7221 6119

Bayley & Sage
60 High Street,
Wimbledon Village,
London SW19 5EE
Tel 020 8946 9904
www.bayley-sage.co.uk

Raoul's Deli
8–10 Clifton Road,
London W9 1SS
Tel 020 7289 6649

East Dulwich Deli
15–17 Lordship Lane,
London SE22 8EW
Tel 020 8693 2525

THE SOUTH

Williams & Brown
28a Harbour Street,
Whitstable, Kent CT5 1AH
Tel 01227 274 507

ACKNOWLEDGEMENTS

We would like to thank our parents for all their help and support both with this book and with Fino, also Robsy Hart for her patience and good humour during our kitchen trashing sessions, and finally the staff at Fino, both past and present, for all their hard work, which has made Fino the place it is today.